The Land That Isn't There

The Land That Isn't There

An Irish Adventure

LEONARD WIBBERLEY

IVES WASHBURN, INC.

New York

FOR CHRISTOPHER

*who had to stay home as the man
of the house.*

Eternal is the fact that the human creature born in Ireland and brought up in its air is Irish. Whatever variety of mongrel he or she may derive from, British or Iberian, Pict or Scot, Dane or Saxon, Down or Kerry, Hittite or Philistine: Ireland acclimatises them all. I have lived for twenty years in Ireland and for seventy-two in England; but the twenty came first; and in Britain I am still a foreigner and shall die one.

—GEORGE BERNARD SHAW

CONTENTS

The Land That Isn't There

JOURNEY WITH A SAINT

1. ONE day my son Kevin, who is nine, came to me and said "Daddy, why are you an Irishman?" Kevin was not named after St. Kevin of Glendalough, who died in peace A.D. 618, but after Kevin Barry, who was hung by the Black and Tans.

At the time this question was put to me I was driving a covered wagon across the American west and worried about the condition of my mule Celeste. She had a harness gall on her neck and the flies had got at it, and I didn't think she would last until we made the sink of the Humboldt.

"Huh?" I said.

"Why are you an Irishman?"

"Look, Kevin," I said, "I'm writing a book about the pioneers going west, and I'm having trouble with a mule. If I don't get this book written there is going to be a very unhappy Christmas around this house. So don't bother me with questions about why I'm an Irishman. Just be grateful that I am and go away and play."

This is not the way to bring up children according to the articles in the Sunday supplements but it is the way I raise

3

my kids—Kevin, Patricia, Christopher, Arabella, and Rory O'Connor.

Kevin went away, and I eyed the flies on the mule and thought about the distance to the sink of the Humboldt, and after a harrowing journey I finally got my wagon through to Sacramento, made a lot of money out of farming, and then fought through the Civil War and wound up married.

That is the way with writers. They are never really there. They're listening to the rumble of the death carts through London during the Great Plague and picturing the pale stripped bodies jolting on the top in the moonlight, or flinging a war hammer at Attila the Hun when they should be mowing the lawn or answering the intelligent questions of their intelligent kids in a kindly and adult manner.

After the book was done, I remembered that Kevin had asked me why I was an Irishman, and I began to reflect on this.

I was born in Ireland, to be sure. But that was a mere pretense at an answer. What is Ireland? It is the most westerly island of Europe if you discount Iceland. It is a forlorn island, very beautiful in parts and very wild in others. It is drenched by rain and drenched by sunshine, which alternate like sin and repentance. It is a place full of legends and holy wells and ruined monasteries and round towers.

It is a place where the taxi drivers of Dublin maintain a shrine in the middle of their cab rank to the Virgin Mary and tip their hats to the statue of Parnell, who was a roaring Protestant. It is a place where swans are revered because they are the daughters of Lir (Shakespeare took that legend and out of it wrote his play *King Lear*). It is a place where asses have a cross of darker hair on their backs because it was on the back of an ass that Christ rode into Jerusalem on Palm Sunday.

4

All that is Ireland. But it is more than that, too. It is a place where the Rosary is recited during a storm for the protection of the household, the beads clicking as the rain lashes against the windows and the lightning appalls the night. It is a place where people are conscious of the supernatural all around them—guardian angels and saints and Other Beings neither of heaven nor of hell. It is a place where a lone magpie crossing the road must be civilly addressed or you will have bad luck all morning, and it is also a place that raises the greatest horses in the world, the merriest foxes, and the plumpest geese.

I reflected then that all this and a thousand other things were what made me an Irishman. Kevin had not experienced any of them; for, since he was born in America, his background was entirely different from mine. There was, of course, no reason why he should except that he was curious about why I was an Irishman, and I wanted him to know something about my own boyhood at first hand. Explanations would not serve. Experience was needed. The obvious thing to do was to take him to Ireland and show him.

I had made one short visit to Ireland with my whole family, but it was not enough. So I determined to return again taking with me Kevin and my daughter Tricia, who was seven. The rest of my family could not come, for my wife Hazel was to have a baby and did not feel up to the journey. But she encouraged me to go, taking Kevin and Tricia with me, until eventually it was decided that we three would spend two months in Ireland and that we would fly there since neither Tricia nor Kevin had been in an airplane before.

And so we went.

There was a saint on the airplane that took us to Ireland. Nobody had to tell me this because I could see it in her face—

a look of holiness that made her very beautiful. She was old and white-haired and frail and halfway to heaven already, I thought, though in the place where we waited to board the plane she was attended by a fat grandson in a sweatshirt who was chewing a cud of gum.

"The leprechauns will be waiting for you, Grandma," said the fat grandson, and it was proof of her sanctity that she did not brain him on the spot with the thick stick she carried in her thin lap. Instead she just smiled and endured this piece of brash vulgarity. While he kept on about leprechauns, I could almost count the additional days in purgatory he would have to endure for tormenting this holy woman.

Eventually it was time to board and she was wheeled out onto the tarmac by her grandson with the aid of two stewardesses (the temperature was 99 in the shade). The chair had to be lifted up the stairs to the plane, and so she was raised up slowly like an offering to God—as if she was ascending into Heaven. And I believe that that was what happened to her. For when I got aboard the plane myself, the saint was not there. I fancy that when she got to the top of the stairs some angels had taken over from the fat youth with his cud of gum and raised the frail woman past the plane and into the vault of Heaven. That would, of course, have been a miracle, but miracles happen all the time and are not to be either denied or doubted because people were having their boarding passes checked and so were not looking.

There had been a mixup about my plane reservation entirely as a result of my own stupidity. I had made the reservations three months in advance and paid for the tickets at that time. In doing this I had offered my fellow countrymen a deep affront. I had assumed they could be tied to a plan—the plan consisting of their holding three seats for me on an airplane that was to leave New York three months later.

6

Of course, Irish Air Lines had rejected this piece of presumption, this effort to make the Irish predictable and infallible. When I got to New York from my home in California there were no seats for me at all, and only after much telephoning backward and forward from New York to Los Angeles did I manage to get on the plane.

Still, we got three seats together, Kevin near the window and Tricia in the middle so if she got frightened she could hold on to me.

A buxom stewardess, sweltering in a skirt of Donegal tweed, offered us some chewing gum, which Tricia declined by opening her mouth to demonstrate that she already had some. We all fastened our safety belts. The engine roared. The plane lumbered out onto the runway and stayed there a while, taking a look around to see if the various American, Dutch, British, French, and Italian planes had left any kind of a hole for our Irish plane to fly up into in the sky and go to Ireland where it was cooler.

Eventually it spotted an open place and plunged off toward it. The engine noises increased. Tricia dug her fingers into my arm and closed her eyes. Kevin gave me a look of fright and a woman with two babies in the seat across from me leaned back, her infants in her arms and her lips moving. Because I was familiar with what she was saying, I could lip-read the words. They were "Holy Mary, Mother of God, pray for us sinners, now and at the hour of our death. Amen."

Finally we were up in the sky, and a conversation took place between Tricia and Kevin to which I was not privy.

"She is not, is she?" Kevin asked me at the end of this. It is a peculiarity of his that he thinks I know what is going on in his head all the time. I suppose that he pictures me so vividly in his mental conversation that it comes as a shock to realize that I'm not there at all.

7

"I don't know," I replied vaguely. "Why don't you ask her?"

"O.K.," said Kevin, and he beckoned the stewardess as she passed by.

"My father wants to know if you're wearing diapers?" he said.

"Damnation, boy," I roared, "I don't want to know anything of the sort."

"Well you said to ask her," said Kevin.

"I did not," I snarled.

The stewardess was very sweet. "Does the little girl want to go to the ladies' room?" she asked.

"Yes," said Tricia, squirming between embarrassment and discomfort. The stewardess took her there. I turned on Kevin.

8

"Listen," I said. "What do you mean by asking the stewardess that question and saying I wanted to know."

"Well, Tricia said that all the women would have to wear them because it takes a long time to get to Ireland."

"And what about the men?" I roared. "Did you see me swaddling myself in diapers when I left the hotel this morning?"

"Oh, well, men have more control," said Kevin. And having asserted this point he got up and went to the men's room.

It takes five or six days on a ship to get to Ireland. On an airplane it takes an eternity. You sit and smoke and try to read or sleep and listen to the babies crying. You look out at the clouds below and wonder how anything so beautiful could at the same time be so wretchedly dull. You get accustomed to the noise and you watch the blue flame from the exhaust of the engine and come to the conclusion that you're trapped in eternity, and going nowhere at all.

In this eternity of traveling nowhere I began to think about Ireland and reflect that it isn't really anywhere at all. It is a remote place halfway between heaven and earth, like Shangri La or Bali Hi or Ultima Thule. It is one of the few places on earth where the whole population really believe, beyond doubt or quibble, in the immortality of the soul, which I decided was probably the reason my plane reservations got lost. If earthly life is but a second in the eternal life of the individual, who will one day be raised from the dead and go to heaven, it is nothing but foolishness to concern oneself about misplaced airplane tickets.

Here, I reflected, is the key to what is called Irish impracticality. Essentially the Irish are the truly practical people of the earth, concentrating on immortality and refusing to take seriously the need for keeping appointments and not letting the toast burn. Conversely, those people

9

who are never late for appointments, who always know the state of their bank balances, whose clothes are neat and houses abnormally tidy, are likely to be pagans believing their present life the only one they have.

"Pagans," I said aloud, for when I am thinking in this manner I sometimes speak my thoughts, which seems to help make them firmer. "They're all pagans."

"Don't worry about my Daddy," said Tricia, who was kneeling on the seat, the better to address a passenger behind. "He's just talking to himself. He writes books."

"The poor man," said the woman thus addressed. "It must be a terrible strain."

"No," said Tricia who loves company and will strike up a bright conversation with anybody without even a pretext. "It isn't very hard for *him*. But *we* all have to keep quiet."

I was conscious that though I was being eyed with considerable disfavor, I was defenseless. If I told Tricia to sit down and shut up, it would only confirm the suspicions of my harshness which she had already awakened. On the other hand, knowing Tricia, if I permitted her to continue, she would lay all my bad points in the lap of the sympathetic listener behind.

Kevin came to my rescue. "Sit down, big mouth," he said to Tricia, and then to adjust the score for me with the passenger behind, he popped his head over the seat and said, "One of my Daddy's books is being made into a movie."

"Oh, pipe down, the two of you," I said. "Cripes, can't I have even a little privacy?"

"Well, it was because you said everybody was pagans," said Tricia, sulkily examining her hands. Then she stole a look at me to see how I reacted, and smiled like a little wanton.

10

I returned, sulkily, to the contemplations of Ireland, wincing at the hackneyed phrases about the island of saints and scholars, and the little bit of heaven that fell out of the sky one day, and all the roaring nonsense about leprechauns and fairy raths and shamrocks and the Shawn Van Vocht which is really the *Seanbhean Bocht,* meaning the poor old woman. The truth, putting these nauseous sentimentalities aside, is that it is the last remaining home of the Celts, who once controlled the greater part of Europe from the Rhine to the coast of Portugal. That isn't quite true, either. The Scots are Celts and so are the Welsh and the people of Cornwall to a degree (they had their own language up to fifty years ago), and also the people of Brittany, and some say the Basques. But Ireland is the only place where the Celts still govern themselves—the last homeland, then. Into this island they had been driven in a warfare against other peoples which has lasted two thousand and more years, if rightly reckoned. So Ireland is the remaining refuge of a prehistoric race, and because it is so small and on the very edge of what had then been the world, it has not been caught in the various streams of change which affected other countries of Europe.

This is not, of course, to say that all the Irish are pure Celts. There are older strains among them of pre-Celtic people, and newer influences as well. But the greater part of the population is predominantly Celt and the Celtic strain has always quickly transformed any infusion of Saxon or Norman blood. For this reason Ireland has retained its myths and legends and sagas longer than other nations of Europe. England, for instance, was constantly invaded and its folk stories forgotten.

The English, of course, do have the legend of Arthur, but that is a memory that goes back to Celtic times, for Arthur

11

was a Celtic figure, not an Anglo-Saxon or Norman. The Welsh, protected by their mountains, fared better and retain many of the old folk tales, some of which are similar to the Irish. But in Ireland the land abounds in folk tales which are known to all the children and in parts are still told by storytellers to fireside gatherings.

So what is unique about Ireland, I reflected, is that it is populated by a people whose untangled roots go back into prehistory, and prehistory therefore has a large influence on its life and attitude. And as for leprechauns and *si* (fairies), they are the remnants of the old gods, overthrown or rendered harmless by the advent of Christianity, though still privately and secretly respected.

Having made this tidy summary of the essence of Ireland, I settled down to sleep and, of course, was immediately offered dinner. Actually, I got no sleep that night. The plane was full of returning Irish men and women, patriotically traveling on an Irish aircraft back to Ireland, and they visited with each other up and down the aisle. Then, of course, the sun rose at what was, for me, three o'clock in the morning, at which unseasonable hour I was offered breakfast. And still we plunged on through the sky above the beautiful monotonous clouds, flying, as I had concluded earlier, absolutely nowhere. But after a while the clouds thickened and darkened, and a big man from Clare who had been informed by Tricia that I was going to Ireland to buy a castle so I could have a quiet place in which to write, looked out of the window and said, "We must be getting near Ireland. It's raining."

We fastened our safety belts and slipped into the clouds, and the wings of the plane were immediately darkened with rain. Then Ireland floated up out of the world to meet us—

13

a place of tiny fields and lilliput roads and lakes with faces as bright as hope.

I glanced around at my fellow passengers. Half of them were smiling and biting their lips, and the other half were dabbing their eyes, and the woman with the two babies said, "We're there, thanks be to God."

DEEP IN CONNEMARA

2.   THE place in which we were to live in Ireland was on the coast of Connemara in the heart of the Irish-speaking part of the country, which is called the Gaelteach. I had selected this village because it was remote and close to the sea, and these are conditions I enjoy. The villagers had once been fishermen but there is no real fishing done there now, though there is still a little harbor to protect the boats from the Atlantic storms. Some men support themselves by farming, and those who have no taste for this or no land of their own work on the roads or repair houses or do something of this nature. The greater number of the young men emigrate to England or to the United States and some even go to Australia. So do the young women. Therefore the village is full of the middle-aged and the elderly and children. I will call the village Killron, but that is not its name. To give the real name would be an invasion of the privacy of the people in it who are my friends.

Killron's only street follows the contour of the bay, coming in as a road off the boglands. You travel this road from Galway, and when you have passed Oughterard you come

to the boglands—places of alternating light and shadow with always the sense of a great wind blowing over them. Mountains rise from the bogs—desolate and old and seemingly of enormous height and size, though none of them top two thousand feet. They are the Maamturks, and beyond them, the Twelve Pins. Occasionally there are lakes and usually an island or two, high with trees, in the center. Lakes, islands, mountains, bogs are all lonely. The road seems happy only when it leaves the bogs to turn toward Killron and become the thoroughfare of the village.

Killron is not a pretty place, closely viewed. The houses are built in a row, shoulder to shoulder, seemingly huddled together against the weather. The roofs are of depressing slate, and few of the houses are blessed by a garden before them. Yet the village is set in enchanting scenery with a view of the Twelve Pins. Across the bay is an island and further down the bay toward the Atlantic are several more, while back of the village is a mountain. And when we

16

arrived, a tangle of wild red roses was growing over the harbor wall.

This, then, was where we were to live for a month—Kevin and Tricia and I—in a tiny Irish village cut off from the world on one side by a moat of boglands and mountains, and facing the Atlantic on the other side, with the nearest land some three thousand miles across the water. Later we would move to another village to the south—a gentler place less than twenty miles from Galway.

We found the house I had rented and looked it over. It was so clean that I thought of forty maids with forty mops scrubbing for forty years. Upstairs there were three bedrooms with linoleum on the floor, and a large bathroom. The bathroom had only a washbasin and a commode—no bath nor shower. There was no hot water. Downstairs was a tiny sitting room, a large kitchen with a kitchen range, and another kitchen with a gas stove in it burning Calor gas supplied from a replaceable container.

The grate in the large kitchen glowed like a furnace and I smelled something which I had forgotten about for more than thirty years—burning peat. The smell is something like hay but with a richness to it—somewhere between hay and hot chocolate. Up to that moment I had been rather tense and nervous because of the long drive from Limerick in a tiny rented car which we called Peanut, after a sleepless night on an airplane. But when I smelled the burning peat it was like balm on a quivering wound. I sat down in a chair and enjoyed the fire.

Kevin and Patricia meanwhile did some exploring. This consisted of taking a quick look around the house and then going next door to see who lived there. The people who lived there of course were my landlords—Tom and his wife and

17

children. There were five of these children, I discovered—
Marie, Josephine, Jackie, Noel and Paddy.

When I missed the children I found them in Tom's kitchen
eating soda bread and drinking tea (which they had never
drunk before), and chattering away like magpies about the
plane trip from New York.

"Come on in, boss," said Tom. He was a big man, clad
in a gray fisherman's jersey and rough tweed trousers. He
introduced me to his wife, who immediately sat me down
at the table and insisted that I also take tea. Tea consisted
of soda bread and ham and boiled eggs and marmalade—a
huge meal served under the pretense that it was a snack.
The kitchen was low-ceilinged and plastered and washed
down with a cool blue. There was an open fire—nothing more
than a hearthstone and a chimney where several turfs were
burning, giving off their delicious smell. Over the fire a pot
was placed with some burning turfs on the lid. It was all
familiar to me, though utterly strange to my children. Yet
they seemed entirely at home in this kitchen which had never
known a gas stove nor a refrigerator nor a dishwasher nor
a garbage disposal unit.

Out of the pot on the fire, after a while, Tom's wife—a
handsome woman with healthy red cheeks—scooped a huge
loaf of soda bread.

This was for me to take, she said, and would not listen
to any protest.

"Would you like a lobster for your dinner?" Tom asked.
I said I would.

"I'll have one for you tomorrow. Maybe you'd like to go
over to the island."

"He has a boat," said Kevin, and I suspected that this
little excursion had been arranged before my arrival.

18

"It's not a long pull," said Tom. "Less than a mile. That's all. And the wind is on a good point."

I said I'd like to go.

"They've got hens," said Tricia. "One of them has only got one leg. Noel fell in the water and was nearly drowned. Tom had to pull him out and it was in the papers even in America."

Well, I thought as this chatter continued, there's one thing about Ireland that hasn't changed. You are never among strangers. I rounded the children up, unpacked, and got them ready for bed.

They were in need of a bath, both of them, but there was no bath in the house. On the top of the kitchen range three big kettles hissed contentedly, each of them containing perhaps half a gallon of boiling water. I went into the smaller kitchen and found what I was looking for—a large galvanized tub hanging by a nail on the wall.

"Come on," I said, putting the tub down before the peat fire. "You are going to have a bath."

"In that?" asked Kevin.

"Yes."

"Did you used to take a bath in a tub when you were a boy?"

"Of course he did," said Tricia, who was wriggling out of her clothes. "He wasn't dirty all his life."

I poured some boiling water from one of the kettles into the tub while Tricia hopped around as naked as a peeled stick, saying "ooh" and "ah" at the thunder of the water and the rising steam. I knew exactly how she felt, a mixture of fear and excitement. Then I poured in some cold, tested the mixture with my hand and told her to get in. She got in by centimeters. Then she sat down in the tub, warmed

19

by the water and the fire, which threw a golden light on her slender shoulders.

A few of the techniques of bathing in a tub began to come back to me. "Don't put your elbows outside," I said, "the water will run down them onto the floor. Wash your feet and legs first and then kneel down and wash the rest of you. Put the soap on the floor beside the tub."

Kevin was sitting in a chair opposite me (the tub being between us), examining his toes in a dreamy manner as if he had just discovered them and was but mildly interested in them.

20

"That stuff they burn in the fire," he said. "Where do they get it from?"

"It's peat. Only the Irish call it turf. They get it out of the bogs."

"All they want?"

"Yes."

"Do they have to pay for it?"

"They pay about a dollar fifty a year, and a part of the bog is laid out for them and they can dig all the turf they want."

"Can I go out on the bog?"

"Sure. Sometime. Get into the tub now and have a bath."

He got in and announced the water was not hot enough. I poured some more in from the kettle and he sat down gingerly. Hunched up, he began to examine himself for any interesting scabs, but to his disappointment found none. Tricia knelt down between my knees to have her hair dried and brushed. She had got her nightie and Kevin's pajamas, for she is very good at these domestic details.

After a while Kevin got out of the tub, and it was only when he had dried himself before the fire and put on his pajamas that I discovered he hadn't washed at all but just lain soaking and dreaming in the hot water. Oh, well. I'd done the same thing myself. They said their prayers and I packed them off to bed and went out into the street to stand by the sea wall and breathe the soft air. The night was so dark that I had to grope my way to the sea wall, for the street lights in the village had been extinguished.

The sea was a vague luminescence before me, and the darker place beyond it, the island of Inishnee. It seemed to undulate a little, as if it floated on the barely visible water. I could hear a gentle tinkling as the tide crept into the bay, rolling the little stones upon each other. There was a hoarse bird-cry and a whirr of wings in the blackness and then silence again except for the sound of the creeping tide.

After a while I became aware of a whiteness on the sea wall a little way off on my right and made out Tricia in her nightie and Kevin in his pajamas sitting there staring at the island. A car came down the street illuminating us and I wondered what the driver would think to see a man with a beard and two children in their nightclothes sitting on the wall in the pitch black looking out to sea.

Probably, I decided, he wouldn't think anything at all except to reflect that he was in Ireland.

EELS AND FOXES

3.　　　　THE next day we went in the boat to Inishnee. Tom took the forward pair of oars and his son Noel
and Kevin divided the other pair between them. I sat in
the stern with Tricia, who had decided that for the day
she would be very feminine.

We let out a line with a spinner on the end of it in case
we met a stray mackerel, and were hardly clear of the pier
before Tom was talking about his boat, to which I found
he was devoted.

"I believe I could go to America in her," he said. "If we
had weather like this we could go all the way without a
drop of trouble. I've had this boat twenty-five years and
there was another man had her before that. Forty years old
she is at least, and as strong as the day she was built. Never
leaked a drop of water yet."

All the time he was talking, there was the merry slap of
the water on the sides of the boat and the thump of the
oars on the gunwales and the swish of them as they met
and left the sea. The boats of the west of Ireland do not
use rowlocks, but thole pins. A wooden peg is inserted in

the gunwale and fits into a hole in a lug on the oar. This, for a fisherman, is a superior arrangement to a rowlock, for he may let go his oars to handle a net or a line or a lobster pot and there is no danger the oar will go over the side as it might with a rowlock.

"What do you call this kind of boat?" I asked.

"A curragh," said Tom. "On the Aran Islands out there they have curraghs that are made of canvas, but we have figured it out here that the ones planked with wood are the best." (Mainland fishermen hold themselves somewhat superior to the men from the offshore islands, whom they think backward.)

"We used to use the canvas curraghs ourselves long ago. But you have only to touch a rock with them and you're holed that very instant. And if you put your foot in the wrong place you'd make a hole, or if you had a big conger

24

eel aboard you'd have a hole in her, trying to kill the eel. Though I knew a man that was out to sea in a curragh and got a hole in the canvas, and he had it repaired in a minute."

"How did he do that?" I asked.

"He took his shirt and plugged the hole with it," said Tom.

"How far out at sea was he?" I asked.

"He was not far out," said Tom. "About three miles."

I was interested by the reference to conger eels, of which I had heard some fearsome tales as a boy. These are perhaps the largest eels in the world and I had been told they could readily bite the bone of a man's leg in two.

"How big do conger eels get?" I asked.

"I've seen them over twelve feet long," replied Tom, "and as thick around the middle as a man's thigh. I remember a fight I had with one of them once when I was not much bigger than Noel there. I had come over to the island alone and was fishing, when I caught an eel. I got him into the boat and he was writhing and whacking away at the sides. I thought to myself, seeing the size of him, that it would be better if he stayed in the ocean and me in the boat for he was all but hammering the planks out of her. I was frightened so bad that I didn't know what to do and kept hitting it with the oar and was afraid that it would bite off my foot. It was the eel made up my mind, for it got over the side and back into the sea."

"Did you leave it there?" asked Kevin.

"I did not," said Tom. "I was frightened of it and I was angry with it for frightening me, at the same time. So I hauled it back in again and the fight started once again for who was going to control the boat. But in the end I got the better of him. I daren't take the big hook out of his mouth, for he'd have had my hand off. So I tied him with the hook still in his mouth to the forward seat, and then

25

I put hooks in his body and tied them all down the boat so that he was stretched the length of it.

"He went the full length of the boat and the boat was over twelve feet long, so that was the size of him. Then I had to row back to the mainland with the eel below me and I was still afraid of putting my feet in the bottom of the boat lest he get loose and bite me. So I had to step from seat to seat when I wanted to move about in the boat to get the anchor up and so on. But at last I got him back. He weighted ten stone (one hundred and forty pounds), and I sold him for seven pounds when I had him ashore. Everyone in the village came down to have a look at him. It was the biggest eel taken that year, though there have been bigger than that caught."

"What's the best way to kill them?" I asked.

"There is a weak spot behind their heads," said Tom. "If you put a knife in the right place, they're dead in a minute. But when I caught my eel I hadn't a knife with me. I was frightened, I can tell you."

Conger eels, at certain times of the year, live under rocks on the seashore, Tom said. They push away the sand from beneath the rock to make room for themselves, so if you find a rock with sand in a mound in front of it you can be sure there's an eel there. He may be only four feet long or he may be twice that length, so you can decide for yourself whether to go after him or leave him alone.

We landed at a little cove on the island and started to climb up over the rocks to the grasslands above. I stopped to look at one of the rock pools among the heavy, yellow hanks of seaweed. There was an almost invisible shrimp sailing along below the surface and a sea anemone and some periwinkles and some limpets. Kevin put his hand in the pool and picked up a purple periwinkle. For a moment I

26

had the curious feeling that it was my hand and that he was me. Tom took a clasp knife and with a quick movement dislodged a limpet from the rock.

"The *bairneachs* are the only creatures in the world that can trap a fox," he said.

"That little thing?" said Tricia in disbelief.

"Well it happened once on this island, and here is the way it was," said Tom. "The fox came down to the shore one day to get a drink of rain water out of a pool. The pools higher up fill with rain water and the ones lower down with sea water. When the fox had had his drink he started to look around for something to eat and saw the *bairneach*, with his shell raised up a little from the rock to cool himself from the heat of the sun. So the fox thought he could flip him over and eat him. He slipped his tongue under the edge of the shell and the moment he did so, the *bairneach* clamped down hard on the rock and had the fox trapped by his tongue. One of the farmers found him."

"What did they do with him?" asked Tricia.

"Cut off his tail," said Tom, "and sold it for three pounds." Tom, I soon found, knew the price of the most unlikely articles.

We went on a little farther, and Tom told me the story of the only fox that ever got to the Aran Islands, which lie off the Connemara coast and are among the most desolate in the world. There is no earth on them by nature, and so earth has to be made by mixing sand with rotted seaweed, on which soil the islanders raise crops of potatoes and corn and a few vegetables. There are no trees on any of the three Aran Islands, which are, for the most part, rocks.

"There never was a fox on the Aran Islands until a few years ago," said Tom. "And then one got into one of the boats that was carrying turf over to the middle island,

Inishmaan. As soon as the boat docked, the fox leaped ashore and it was soon the plague of the whole place, carrying off the few hens and ducks that the islanders were raising for eggs. It killed off most of the dogs too."

"I never heard of a fox killing a dog," I objected.

"Well, he killed them, all right," said Tom. "The people would see the dogs chasing the little red fox, maybe in the sunlight or maybe in the sea mists, over the rocks, and then the dogs would all disappear and their bodies would be found crushed at the bottom of a cliff. Some of the people thought that it wasn't a fox at all that had come to the island but some kind of a spirit. The fox with the dogs behind it would run to the edge of the cliff and then they would all go over it in full cry and the dogs would be killed. But the fox would appear again the next day or maybe a little later. The people began to be afraid of it, I can tell you, for it seemed as if that fox was immortal.

"Then one day one of the islanders was in his curragh fishing off the cliffs and he heard some dogs barking at the top. He looked up and sure enough the fox appeared at the edge, gave a little jump, caught some brambles that grew a few feet down the face of the cliff and swung himself into his burrow which was behind the brambles. But the dogs came over so fast they flew right off the cliff and down to the bottom where they were killed on the rocks beneath.

" 'So that's your little secret,' said the fisherman. 'Well, I know it now, and it is your turn next.' So he climbed up the cliff and cut the brambles until they were only just held together and any little touch would break them through.

"Sure enough, a day or so later, the last two dogs on the island found the fox prowling around and chased it and the fox headed for the cliff and gave his little jump for the clump of brambles. But the brambles gave way, and down he went to the rocks below and was killed with the dogs behind him. So there was neither fox nor dog on the Inishmaan for a while until the islanders brought over some more dogs for company. But they never brought over a fox again, for that one fox had given them more trouble than they cared for."

I have forgotten to say that the pretext for coming over to Inishnee was to see the light which burned night and day on a point of the island as a guide for boats entering the bay and headed for Killron. It was a simple device— a huge oil lamp on the top of a metal pole. There was a reservoir of oil over the wick and this allowed a certain number of drops a minute to fall upon the wick, keeping it alight. At the foot of the light was a multitude of granite boulders, worn smooth by the sea. At one place there was a large basin cut in the granite rock by the action of the waves. It was filled with boulders, each as large and as round as a cannonball. They had been flung up into the depression by the waves and rolled around in it by tide after tide until they were almost perfect spheres. I tried to pick one up but it was too heavy for me.

Tom said if I felt like rowing we could go over to another island, Inishlacken, where there was a great storyteller. The wind had come up a little and the channel was rough, but I said I would like to go.

We got into the curragh again and set off, and a few yards off the shore met the wind and the waves. The waves were long and big. They flung the curragh up into the air so that, sitting in the bow with the oars, at times I was several feet above Tom in the stern and could look down on him.

The tide was against us and there was a wildness to the wind and water in mid-channel. The wind caught the curragh, trying to turn its head off, and the waves broke and hissed around us. With each stroke of the oars we seemed to advance but half a foot. I thought how powerless a man is on the sea. The sea will let him come and go for a little while and then it will toss him around like a cork. It can take big rocks and roll them smooth as marbles and bend in the plates of the largest ships as if they were made of paper. There was a low howl to the wind as we rowed and the water was all green and white.

We rowed for half an hour, then an hour, and then an hour and a half. And finally the sea lessened and we got under a headland of Inishlacken and went ashore in a little harbor where an old *pucán* was rotting by the sea wall.

There are only four families living on Inishlacken now, though there were eighty a few years back. We passed a school house without a roof. School is no longer held on the island. Sheep graze where the children recited their multiplication tables, and the wind howls over the shell of the school. There is an air of melancholy and loneliness about the place, and where there were once little fields there are now only enclosures full of bracken and brambles.

Where had the people gone and why did they go, leaving the little stone houses where they had sat snug before the fire of turfs many a winter night?

We came upon an old man working in his little field of hay. He was going through the cut hay and picking out the stalks of weeds which might make his few cattle sick.

"He's the storyteller," said Tom to me. "Perhaps he will tell us a story." Then he called out to the old man. "Good day," he said.

"Good day," said the man, and came within twenty feet of us and sat on a rock looking us over closely.

"That's a nice little dog you have there," said Tom, nodding

30

to the Wexford Hills sheep dog which had seated itself beside the old man.

"He isn't a patch on his father," said the old man. "I never had to say a word to his father. He knew the work as well as I. He'd fetch the cows for milking without me opening my mouth and he would comfort them when I had to take them in the boat over to the mainland to market. There wasn't a dog like him in the whole world. He died a little time after the great storm."

"It was a terrible storm, that," said Tom.

"It was," said the man. "Do you see that house there now?" pointing to the ruins of a house on a hill perhaps fifty feet above the sea. "That was the house I lived in then, but the storm destroyed it.

"My brother and I stood with our backs to the kitchen door trying to keep the waves out, but it was no good. They flung against the door and broke it off the hinges and in a minute the whole house was under the sea. I had a cow at the time. She was in calf and in the stable a little way

31

up the hill, and when the house had gone I thought of my little cow and how she would be drowned if I didn't save her—and her calf was not yet born though it was due any time.

"So I ran to the stable after the cow. I had to run between the waves, timing myself so as not to be caught by one of them. The stable door was held shut with a big rock and I stooped to move the rock, when a wave came and broke over me and pulled me out to sea. But the next wave put me back ashore again.

"I got the stone away from the door and unloosed the cow. Out she went through the door and got to the high land. She had the prettiest little calf you ever saw a few days later."

I was astonished that the waves, even of a full gale, could have come so high on the island.

"There was not a part of the island they did not reach," said the old man. "It was after that the people left. The roofs had been taken off most of their houses and the doors knocked in and all their belongings gone. There was no food anywhere and no water to drink. Then boats could come over from the mainland, the people left and did not come back again."

"But you did not leave?"

"I did," said the old man. "I had no house. I went to England and then to Wales and then to Scotland and worked forty years. Then I came back and built another house there, higher than the old one, as you can see. I don't think the storm could reach it. But maybe it could."

"Do you know any stories?" asked Tom.

"No," he said, "I don't know any stories."

HOME IS THE SAILOR

4. I HAD bought Kevin a football, to the delight of the rest of the children in the village. They kicked it about the street and very often into the water of the bay beyond the sea wall which bordered one side of the street. If it went a long way out, they had to get a boat and go after it. But more often it did not go very far. They could get it in the shallow water, having first climbed the sea wall and thrown stones at it until it was close enough to be reached.

Several times, however, they kicked it into a lady's garden, and the last time this happened she came out and took the ball, announcing they were not to have it back again.

It was Jackie who told me about this.

I was on the beach looking around for nothing in particular among the rocks and stones when Jackie joined me. "Will ye be going into Galway today?" he asked.

"I may be," I replied.

"Arrah, then," said Jackie, "ye'll be able to buy another football." Sensing that he had been perhaps too precipitous, he handed me a large scallop shell as a particular treasure, for Patricia was collecting them. "Maybe ye could get a ball in Clifden," he added.

"Where's the ball you had?" I asked.

Jackie hitched his ragged little trousers up around his thin waist. "The 'ould biddy in that house yonder took it," he said.

"Did you break one of her windows?" I asked.

"Divil a bit of it," said Jackie. "She's cross-grained, that's all."

"Did you ask her for it back?"

"She said she'd skin us alive," said Jackie with a shudder. He contemplated his trouser buttons. The greatest problem in Jackie's life centers around trouser's buttons, for there are not enough of them to adequately support his pants, and he has no more waist than a golf club, so a belt is out of the question. I suppose that Jackie has seven or eight years of trouser-button trouble ahead of him until he becomes less active and the strain on the buttons is not so great. Or until he grows a waist to provide lodgment for a belt. Now, having looked at his buttons and assured himself they were holding his trousers right, he said, "She'd skin ye alive if ye asked her for it back, too."

The challenge had now been issued and I marveled at the cunning of it.

I could go to the cross-grained lady in the house and demand my son's ball back. Or I could go to Clifden or Galway and buy another one. The children of the village were relying on me to do one or the other. Of course, I could take a third and cowardly way out. I could say that it served them right that they had lost the ball, and be hanged if I was going to buy another one. But if I did that I would lose not only my own self-respect but the respect of the children of the village, especially of Jackie, who had in

34

a remarkably adroit manner presented me with the problem.

So I went to the woman's house and knocked on the door which, like all doors in the village, was open anyway. A very tall elderly man came out slowly. He had silver hair as thick as a boy's and the skin on his face was not rough but as smooth as that of an infant's. He was smoking a pipe. He had no teeth of his own but only a partial upper plate on the left side of his mouth. This was so loose that when he talked, it flopped up and down from upper to lower gums as if he had a stone in his mouth to suck.

"Good day," I said.

"Good day," he replied.

"I wonder if I could get Kevin's football."

"The wife took it," he said with a trace of a smile in his blue eyes. "She will be out directly."

His wife now came to the door. She was tall like her husband. Her face was full of mischief. I do not recall when I have ever seen such a puckish and handsome face. Her hair was gray but her eyebrows were straight and black. She looked at me with the hint of a challenge—I think to see whether I would lose my nerve and back down, or would still ask for the ball.

"Have you Kevin's ball in the house?" I asked.

"I have indeed," she replied. "They were kicking it into my flowers. I said I'd skin every one of them alive."

"So they told me," I replied.

"I would, too," she said. "It's a hard thing to raise flowers around here."

Shortly after baptism, my parents had the good sense to take me to kiss the Blarney stone; so I said I was very fond of flowers indeed and there was some kind of kinship among people, wherever they were from, who liked to raise flowers.

35

"Go away with you," she said, laughing, and came out with the football.

Her husband, sucking both on his partial plate and his pipe, had now seated himself on the low stone wall surrounding the garden, ready for a little conversation.

"You'll be from America?" he asked as an opening gambit.

"Yes," I replied.

"I was there myself," he commented. "I went at the worst time there was and I stayed there twenty-five years."

I was surprised. From so small a village to so distant and different a place. "When did you go?" I asked.

36

"Nineteen twenty-nine," he replied. "It was the time of the depression. I couldn't have hit it worse. It was bitter cold, and a hundred men lining up for one job. It took me three weeks to get a job myself, and when I had it I held on to it for the next quarter of a century."

"How did you get your job?" I asked.

"I think it was because I was the tallest man in the crowd." He looked for a minute at the waters in the bay as if he could see in them the streets of New York of a quarter of a century before.

"Maybe it was because I was in the Navy, too," he said. "I was torpedoed three times. That was in the Great War. The last time I was torpedoed it was in the *Endymion* off the coasts of Bulgaria. We were fighting the Turks and the Bulgarians. I was having a cup of tea with my mates and the whole deck rose up to meet me and the place was full of smoke and flames and broken crockery and men killed. There was twenty of them dead when they got around to counting. Some thought it was an aerial bomb, and some, the Turkish artillery, and some said it was a mine. But it was a torpedo that did it. It ripped open the starboard side amidships and wrapped it over the deck as neat as you'd fold down an envelope.

"Well, when I'd looked around and found I wasn't hurt, I went down to the engine room—that was where I was supposed to go—and closed off the bulkheads to keep the water off of the boilers. We took a heavy list, and the only thing to be done was to flood some of the compartments on the other side so that the ship would straighten up in the water. We straightened her out all right and kept steam on her, but she settled so low in the water that it was plain she would sink. So we beached her on an island and then I joined the Army."

37

"The Army?" I asked.

"Well, it was either that or stay on the island until the Navy came to take us off. They didn't seem to be in any hurry. We were there two weeks and running out of food when the Army sent a couple of launches over and asked for volunteers.

"I wasn't going to rot on that island off the coasts of Bulgaria without any tobacco so I volunteered and joined the Army for a while and got put in the Royal Engineers. But I changed back to the Navy again and stayed there until the war was over. I left in 1929 and started for America. If I'd stayed, in another ten years I'd have got a pension, but I thought to myself that I could make out better as a civilian."

He did not, however, go directly to the United States. Fifteen years' service in the Royal Navy had left him with a considerable nest egg. Indeed it had left him with sufficient to buy a little public house ashore in Halifax, Nova Scotia, where his customers were likely to be seafaring men and he could, like Long John Silver when he owned the Spy Glass Inn at Bristol, get a sniff of the salt air and the tar.

The public house was the undoing of him. His customers were indeed seafaring men, many of them his own bunk mates from the Royal Navy. But between treating them to drinks and joining them himself, he soon ran into debt and had to sell out.

"I was my own best customer," he said with a smile of mischief.

Then he went to Brooklyn, New York, and encountered the depression. As it was, he was lucky. He was only three weeks landing a job tending boilers in a Brooklyn chemical factory, and there he stayed for the next twenty-five years. He bought a house in Brooklyn, and married and had a son.

38

He became a citizen, voted in the elections, and tended steadily to his work and saved his money.

"My wife was the saving of me," he said. "Without her I'd have been off roaming the world. But every Friday I gave her my pay and she handed me over enough for tobacco and a drink or two, and so we lived decently together.

"When World War II came along my son was mad to get into the Navy. There was nothing to do but to sign the papers for him and off he went."

"Did you give him any particular advice?" I asked.

"No," he said. "When I was a young fellow advice was wasted on me and I expected it would be the same with him."

Then his wife died, and he reached sixty-five years of age and was retired. He owned the house in Brooklyn but it was an empty house. There was no work for him to do and no place for him to go.

Well, not quite no place.

There was the village he had been born in back in Ireland. So he sold the house and took passage back again to the village on Galway Bay, exchanging the teeming millions of New York for a place of no more than a few hundred inhabitants. Then he married the handsome pixie-faced woman who had taken Kevin's football, and every week, when he gets his pension from America, he hands it over to her and she gives him enough for tobacco and a drink or two and they live decently together.

"Did you always intend to come back here?" I asked.

He sucked for a while on his pipe and moved the partial upper plate around in his mouth. "I never had an intention that lasted longer than a week," he said. "There's only one place I would like to go back to."

"Where's that?" I asked.

"The island I was torpedoed off, on the coasts of Bulgaria. I'd like to see whether my old ship the *Endymion* is still lying on the beach."

One day I went out on the bog to see how the peat is cut, taking Kevin with me, for he had wanted to go. Tricia stayed with Maria, who said she would show her some little pigs. The bog is not a slough of mud and weeds, but a firm springy mat covered with a rank grass. It feels as you walk upon it as though you were treading on several thicknesses of straw mattress.

The bog is full of mysteries and one of them is how it got there in the first place. It consists of an interweaving of fibrous roots to a depth of several feet—in some places so deep that no bottom has been found. It would appear that there had been an original growth of grasses, and over this other grass had grown, and then other grass again, and so on, layer building upon layer through the ages.

But there is some black substance intermingled with these dead root fibers. Maybe it is earth, but it has a coal-like quality. When it is newly cut and wet, the turf is soft and slippery. But when it has dried out, it is hard.

The boglands seem to have been covered with forests at one time. Stumps and branches and even trunks of trees are often found by the peat diggers. They are not decayed, these forest relics, but are in excellent condition, and seem to be impregnated with a thin oil. The wood of these trees is very hard and heavy and is called either "bog deal" or "bog oak." It will not rot, either in water or left about in weather.

What killed off the trees? There are none of them on the bogs now—not a tree to be seen for miles and miles. There is another mystery of the bog and that is the fairy fire. It is difficult to get the Irish to speak of it because they know you will not believe but think them ignorant.

The fairy fire appears mostly in winter. Walking through the bog of a dark night you will become aware that behind you is a soft cold glow of light. You turn to find your footsteps outlined in fire on the surface of the bog. Sheep grazing around you leave little footprints of fire as they walk, and these fiery prints remain for several seconds before they disappear.

Phosphorescence? That is the explanation of the drawing room and is acceptable and sensible in these surroundings. But when you are out in the loneliness of the bog, with the heavy dark Irish night above and the wind keening over the mountains, with the smell of the old Gaels rising around your feet, phosphorescence will not serve at all. Then you know that this is not phosphorescence but the fairy fire, and a warning to you to get off the bog lest you be seized and never seen again by mortal man. I have never seen the fairy fire, though several in Killron have. Once, when I was a boy, I saw the fairy light. It was pale and flickered a little way above the ground. It was a flame without heat, the ghost of a flame and burned nothing it touched. My science master said, in his ignorance, that it was methane gas.

Out on the bog, I talked to a man who was cutting the turf. He showed me the *slan* with which the turf is cut and also a little pink hairy flower called the sundew which traps flies, and fetches ten dollars in America, or so he believed.

"You are from there?" he asked.

"Yes."

"Were you ever in New York?"

"I was."

"I was there a year myself," he said. "I took a fancy to go there and try my luck and it was the grand time I had of it."

"What did you do there?" I asked.

"I drove one of the big buses around Manhattan for a year. It was the greatest sport in the world."

"I suppose it got on your nerves after a while."

"No," he said. "I'd be at it yet but I had to come home and take care of the farm."

A gray crane flew out of the loneliness of the bog, glided over us and went out over the loneliness of the sea.

"That's a bird will never get fat," said the former New York bus driver, leaning on his turf spade.

"And why not?" I asked.

"Well, it is the big neck on him. When he's flying over the water he sees his shadow and it frightens him and keeps him too nervous to put any weight on." I thought he was joking, but he was in earnest and repeated the statement.

"What do they call it in Irish?"

"*Maan*," he said.

Maan. That would be Mananan, the old pagan god of the sea after whom the Isle of Man is named and also Inishmán in the Aran Islands. In Ireland the old gods live on in new forms.

LAWYERS AND ALLIGATORS

5. ONE morning, shortly after our arrival in Killron, I went out into the street to find the sea wall lined with people who should normally have been at work on their farms or cutting turf on the bog. There were a dozen small cars parked in the road, and Tom explained it was court day and if we went to the court we might hear something interesting.

The court was held in the house next to the one in which I was living. It consisted of but one small room, with a wainscoting of ugly varnished wood reaching halfway up the walls. Against one wall there was a dais, with a long table before it, at which the magistrate sat.

Before and below this was a boxed-off area at which the clerk of the court sat, and he was flanked by the two solicitors, one for the plaintiff and the other for the defendant. The public were catered to by two benches along the walls, but for the most part these were occupied by witnesses and those who had come to have cases tried. So that most of the public, drawn purely by curiosity, had to stand. However, since I was a stranger and therefore a person to be

43

treated with special courtesy, a police sergeant found room for me on the bench next to an old lady whose daughter was in trouble for not attending school. It had been recommended to the court that the daughter be taken from her mother and put in a school of correction in Clifden.

There were five policemen in the tiny courtroom—an inspector, two sergeants and two constables. The first case called was that of Walsh versus Joyce. It was complicated by the fact that, in this country where many people share the same surname, the Joyces were being defended by a solicitor named Walsh and the Walshes were being defended by a solicitor named Joyce. The matter was further confused because Joyce the plaintiff was suing Walsh the defendant for thirty pounds, charging that he had broken the legs of some of his sheep and drowned two others, while Walsh was charging Joyce in a counter suit that his sheep had been trespassing in Walsh's land, for which he claimed fifty pounds damage.

The magistrate, while all this was being explained to him, kept shuffling the papers on his desk in a distracted manner, and was not aided by the fact that the clerk of the court kept passing other papers up to him. There was an exchange of papers of various kinds between them. After a little while, the two either found what they were looking for or tired of the game, for they stopped and addressed themselves to the case.

James Joyce was first sworn in. He was a tall thin man with a frightened nervous face. He had shaved himself so close that the skin over his cheekbones shone in the subdued light of the courtroom.

"Tell the court what happened to you on the morning of May 14," his solicitor said.

"He broke the legs of two of my sheep."

44

"Who broke them?"

"Why, that man sitting right there on the bench." He pointed to the defendant, Peter Walsh, who had a shock of ungovernable hair on his head and bared his teeth in a delighted grin.

"Kindly name the man, for the court."

"He is my cousin, Peter Walsh."

"How did he break the legs of your sheep?"

"Sure, he took a stone and hit them in the legs with it and broke them."

"Did he throw the stone?"

"He did not. He got the sheep and hit them on the legs holding the stone in his hand."

"Did you try to stop him?"

"I called out to him to stop but he did not."

"Did you lay hands on him?"

"I did not. I am afraid of him."

At this the defendant, Walsh, grinned around the courtroom.

"And what happened after that?"

"Well, two days later he broke the legs of two of my other sheep and a lamb as well."

"With a stone?"

"Yes. With a stone."

"And then?"

"Well, a day later he set his dogs on two of my sheep and ran them into the lake and they were drowned."

"And why did he do this?"

"He said they were grazing on his land but they weren't. It was on my own land that they were grazing, and he came into my land to injure my sheep."

"Did he do anything else?"

"He did. He broke down my fence and made two crosses

and put them in the ground. He said he would bury me and my sister under them and we are afraid of him."

There was a little shudder of fear around the courtroom at this, for there was a suggestion of sacrilege in the erection of the two crosses.

The sister was called next. She looked as frightened as her brother—a woman in her fifties with brown hair fringed with gray and a look of being constantly fearful. She said that the man Walsh had often called her bad names and thrown stones at her. She was afraid of him. Once he set his dogs on her when she was taking the cows to be watered, and the cows had had to go without water that day. It was plain from the way she spoke that there was terror in the little valley where these people came from.

The solicitor for the defendant now arose to cross-examine the Joyces. He picked on the sister.

"Did you ever say that the defendant, Mr. Walsh, should be in a mental home?"

"I did not."

"Didn't you give it as your opinion that he would be better off in the care of doctors?"

"I did not."

"I put it to you that a man who goes around breaking the legs of sheep and marking out graves for people who are still alive might be described as mentally unbalanced."

"Objection," cried the solicitor for the Joyces, "my client is not qualified to give an opinion under oath on the mental condition of another."

"Sustained," said the magistrate, who had returned to the little game of shuffling the papers on his desk and passing them back and forth with the clerk of the court.

"Well, then," said the solicitor for the defendant, "I put

46

it to you that you yourself erected the crosses in order to bolster up your own case against the defendant."

"Why would I tear down my own fence to do a thing like that?" countered the witness.

At this point the magistrate recessed the court for lunch, and we went out to the street to discuss the strange doings in the hills where the legs of sheep were broken and crosses put up as a warning to the living.

A man approached and asked whether I was not from California.

"I have two brothers and a sister there," he said. "There are some queer things happen in California. There was a man out there by the name of Murphy. Did you ever hear of him?"

"No," I said.

"Well, he was a man who was helping to lay the railroad tracks. And there were a lot of Italians laying the railroad tracks, too, and taking the work away from the Irish. So Murphy got some dynamite and put it under the track that the Italians had laid and blew it all up and killed a whole lot of them, God rest their souls. He was killed himself and it was a good thing, for otherwise he would have been hanged for sure."

The story was true, but it wasn't the Italians that the Irish had blown up but the Chinese. Chinese laborers had been hired to lay the transcontinental tracks from San Francisco east and the Irish were laying them from the Mississippi west. The work was paid by the mile, and when the two gangs met in the wilds of Nevada, the Irish dynamited the Chinese camp so they could go on laying track. I had no time, however, to explain this to the man, because he was talking about a brother he had in Australia. He talked fast,

47

as if he had only a little time to impart this knowledge, and it was very important that he should get it out.

"There was an Irishman in Australia by the name of O'Hara," he said. "Did you ever hear of him?"

"No," I replied.

"Well, he was a famous man. He did not want to work at all and decided that he would get an alligator to work for him."

He paused for dramatic effect.

"What did he do?" I asked, seizing the bait.

"He got a little alligator and made it as tame as a cat. It would follow him around like a pet and do tricks for him. Then he took it into Sidney and walked down the street with the alligator behind him, and the people would flock to see the tame alligator, and he made his fortune by it until the police interfered and made him put a muzzle on it.

"The country is full of alligators," he rushed on, determined to cram me with as much information about alligators as he could during the luncheon recess. "Do you know why that is?"

"No," I said.

"Well, it's because they have put all the black fellers on reservations. When they were going around wild they used to get the alligator's eggs and eat them. But now that they're all cooped up like the Indians in America, there is no one to eat the alligator's eggs and the place is thick with them."

He paused for just long enough to suck in a breath and plunged on.

"There was a little girl in Australia that used to have to go to school on a pony. She had to cross a little stream. It was broad, mind you, but shallow enough for the pony to go over. The place was full of alligators. Well, one time the

48

pony came home without the little girl and they knew that she had fallen off and an alligator had got her.

"There was a gang working in the neighborhood putting down a road and her father got some gelignite from them. He found the bank where the alligator had its nest and would be nursing the little girl."

"Nursing her?" I cried.

"Sure they don't eat them right away but keep them under their bellies for a day or two to make them tastier. He put the gelignite down there and blew up the bank and killed the alligator. But every afterwards that pony would not go near the water at all. They tell me the Indians are dying off in America."

"Some of the tribes are increasing," I said.

"The Irish are like the Indians," said the man. "They do not like to stay in one place but love to roam about. But you can't roam about in Ireland because the climate is so bad. Still we do the best we can, moving from one place to another. It is a hard thing to get an Irishman to stay in one place. I think it would kill him in the end. You were never in Borneo?"

"No."

"I've a mind to go to Borneo," he said. He looked down the bay, from which he would set out to Borneo if he ever went there. "I saw a picture about Borneo," he said, "or maybe it was about India. It is all the same thing. Full of wild people."

The court had by now reassembled and the magistrate was once more fiddling with the papers and passing some of them back and forth to the clerk. To my surprise, the man who had buttonholed me in the street and filled me full of lore about alligators now appeared before the bench on a charge of leaving a dead sheep unburied on his land. It

49

seemed that he was a veteran of court appearances, being constantly summoned by the police on one charge or another.

"Have you a solicitor?" asked the magistrate.

"I have not," said the man. "Your Honor knows that the police pull me into court so often that if I were to hire a solicitor I would be without a penny in the world. Besides," he added, looking pointedly at the two solicitors who were in the courtroom, "I know as much about the law as any of them, having been in court as often as they have and with more at stake. I will ask Your Honor to dismiss the case against me."

But this was not to be done without the hearing of evidence first, and one of the police was sworn in. The police in Ireland are required to give their testimony in Gaelic, which is of course the official language of the country. But whether it is the official language or not, few speak Gaelic in daily life, most of them using English. The policeman testified about the sheep in Gaelic, and the clerk of the court, still passing his papers, translated to the accused. The sheep had died and the man had been told to bury it, but he had left it several days (perhaps because he thought an alligator would come along and dispose of it), and so he had been summoned.

The defendant plunged into the fray. To be sure the sheep had died. He did not deny that for a moment. It was a hard loss to a man with as little money as he for a sheep to die on him. He had been out on the bogs cutting turf (footing turf is the expression) and he had left his spade out there. In any case, he could not bury the sheep until he got the fleece off it because it would be too bulky to bury. And in any case, he hadn't his spade with him. And furthermore, there were only eight inches of soil on his farm and how was he to bury a sheep in eight inches of soil? And hadn't a neighbor of his once thrown a dead calf in the bay and the calf had floated out with the tide and gone ashore on the island? And then hadn't the police arrested the man and charged him in court and fined him until his brother had to go to America to earn the money to pay the fine? And wasn't the whole policy of the government to keep the Irish people in Ireland and prevent them from emigrating? And how did they expect to keep the Irish in Ireland when the police were always after them to bury sheep that had died on their land?

This all came out in a torrent, with only a fraction of a second of silence every now and then in which the defendant sucked in a breath like a thirsty man drinking water.

"Well," asked the magistrate at the end of it, "what has been done with the sheep?"

Well, said the defendant, he'd gone to the bog and fetched his spade, found a piece of land deep enough to bury it and had done so. The police knew that he had buried it and they had no right to bring a case against him. A man had never been brought into court before for failing to bury a sheep.

The magistrate produced the legal code covering the burying of sheep and read it. The maximum fine for failure to dispose of a carcass was five pounds.

"Five pounds," cried the defendant, looking wildly around. It was plain his next stopping place would be Borneo. But the magistrate smiled, and after consulting with the police inspector, said that he would impose only a nominal fine.

"But I have not a penny to my name," cried the defendant. "And I buried the sheep. They know that I buried the sheep for I went to the barracks and told them myself. That was after I had taken the fleece off her and gone to the bog to get my spade."

Well, there would be a nominal fine anyway, said the magistrate, but he would not impose it until next September. Would the defendant be in the court next September?

"I will not, Your Honor," said the defendant.

"Then the police will let you know what the fine is," said the magistrate, and returned to the vexed case of the Joyces and the Walshes with the sheep that had broken legs, and the sheep that had been drowned, and the two terrible crosses that had been put up to warn the Joyces they were marked for death.

I was very interested to see how he would dispose of this case, for it was plain that one or other of the parties had perjured themselves, though it had been done with remarkable fervor and frequent references to hopes of gaining heaven.

He disposed of it readily enough by fining both parties. The Joyces were fined for allowing their sheep to trespass on the lands of Mr. Walsh. And Walsh was fined for injuring the Joyces' sheep, though it was plain he could not have broken their legs for they were walking around afterwards, and also for erecting the crosses on their land.

Having imposed the fines, the magistrate expressed the hope that since the two were cousins, they would compose their differences and live together in the future like good neighbors.

But there seemed scant hope of this, for they began immediately to accuse each other of further misdeeds, so that the lawyer for the Joyces had to hustle them out of the court, beating the brother with a roll of newspapers.

As for the old woman with the daughter it had been recommended should be taken away from her, this trial was conducted in Gaelic, since the old woman was a Gaelic speaker. But there were complications, for the Gaelic she spoke was her mother tongue, and different from that of the police and the magistrate who had learned it out of a book. The upshot was that if the girl would attend school regularly she could remain with her mother. But if she did not, she would be taken from her and put in the children's home in Clifden.

"Why doesn't the mother send her daughter regularly to school?" I asked Tom when the court had finished its proceedings.

"Because they teach the girl Gaelic and the old woman thinks it's a waste of time," said Tom.

Outside the court the man who had been found guilty for not burying a sheep, buttonholed me once more.

"Am I to be fined because a sheep dies on me and I have no spade to bury it and no land deep enough to bury it on?" he cried. "Is there any justice in that? You are a stranger: do you think I have been fairly handled? I will sell my farm and go away." And off he went down the road, headed for Borneo, I suppose.

SUCCORED BY A HEN

6. ENTIRELY as the result of the kindness of the postmistress at Killron, we ran out of money when we had been but a few weeks in Ireland. I had made some heavy purchase of things I wished to send to Hazel for herself and the other children, and had also bought a second-hand car of which I will say more later, and my balance at the Munster and Leinster bank in Galway was getting low.

This bank is housed in a building which was part of the castle of the Lynch family. Hundreds of years ago a certain Judge Lynch had condemned his own son to death and, public sympathy being with the youth, no one could be found in the city to hang him. The father had therefore hung his son himself from a window of the castle, and this stern, summary justice was known thereafter as *lynching*, the word being taken to the United States by Irish immigrants, where the practice was eagerly seized upon by the natives of those parts and indeed is not unknown even today.

Anyway, my bank balance being lower than was comfortable, I wrote to Hazel asking her to send some more money.

54

I enclosed some sketches I had made and gave the letter to Kevin with instructions to send it airmail.

It was the duty of the postmistress to charge one shilling and threepence extra if a letter weighed a fraction over an ounce. Irish postmistresses do not like to do this. It seems unfair to have to pay a whole shilling and threepence extra if a letter weighs the merest scruple more than an ounce, and no one is likely to attain heaven by charging one and threepence for the extra word of love a man might be sending his wife thousands of miles away in California. Kevin said that she weighed the letter carefully several times, clucking over it, and it was the merest tittle over the proper weight. She could not, however, bring herself to charge the extra postage, and so sent the letter with her blessing and a single one-and-threepence stamp.

It went sea mail.

The days sped by and no money arrived and my bank balance dwindled. Initially, I was not greatly concerned. I had allowed plenty of time for the receipt of additional funds. But when the days added up to a week, and the week to a fortnight, and the fortnight to three weeks, matters became serious.

I kept running into Galway to inquire casually whether any money had arrived for me, and was told that none had. Eventually I could not go into the bank without feelings of depression and guilt, and it seemed to me the bank staff were keeping an eye on me when I went near the pens or the stationery.

When I had only a few pounds left, I sent a cable. The cable brought no response for several days. (Hazel, it turned out later, was away visiting friends.) Finally the day arrived when I had but two pounds left.

In this situation Kevin began to take the keenest interest

in the hens. He liked them all and had names for every one of them, and at times I would find him with a plump red hen, matronly and content in his hands, smoothing her feathers and talking to her before the fire. After meals he took the leftovers from our table and distributed them to the hens, scolding those who jostled too hard for the food. In return for his kindness, and in view of our impoverished condition, he expected the hens to produce a few more eggs until Hazel came back from the luxurious home in which she was lolling, eating steaks and french-fries, and sent us some money.

One morning, missing him, I went out to the yard to find him squatting down outside the henhouse, peering into it.

"Hush," he said.

"What the devil are you doing?" I demanded.

"Pegleg's laying an egg," he said, "and I'm waiting."

In a little while Pegleg hopped out of the henhouse and Kevin hopped in. He emerged with a large white egg which he gave me for my breakfast.

Well, I suppose that should have cheered me up; but it didn't. It seemed to me that despite all my labors I was reduced to dependency on the generosity of a one-legged hen, and the indignity was more than could be borne. And when I reflected that Hazel, had she known how dependent I was on this one-legged hen, would probably say it was to teach me humility, I roared aloud in agony and kicked a couple of chairs. I swore if I ever got any money again, I would keep it in an old sock so I wouldn't have to go crawling timidly to a bank where a man had hung his own son, and petition the cashier for it.

When I'd calmed down, I apologized to Kevin and Patricia, and he said it was all right. His mother had told him I was

likely to blow up, and not to pay any attention, because if I didn't blow up, I wouldn't be myself.

So I went outside and swore at the hens and came back and made an omelette of the egg, and we ate it for breakfast. After that Kevin arranged privately with Pegleg to lay an egg a day without my knowing it so I wouldn't feel humiliated by my dependency, and this he did.

But we were still without money.

One day Kevin reminded me that I had promised to take him to a sports event being given in a neighboring village. I groaned. There would be an admission charge of some kind and this was no time for luxuries.

57

"You promised," he said. I certainly had, but reckoned him an unfeeling brute for reminding me.

"Okay," I said. "You and Tricia get into the car." And I fingered my sole remaining pound. When I went out to the car myself, Kevin was inside and so was Tricia, and so also were Marie, Josephine, Jackeen, Noel and Paddy and two other children with whom I was but vaguely acquainted.

"I invited them," said Tricia, who loves to play Lady Bountiful and has an enormous belief in my ability to foot the bill.

"How am I to pay the admission for them all?" I hissed to Kevin. He was embarrassed and gave a hopeless shrug of his shoulders, and the nine children who had somehow got into the little Morris 10 looked at me in miserable silence. There was nothing I could do but to drive on, spend my carefully hoarded pound on admission to the sports event, and rely on the generosity of the hens for future sustenance. I had given up on Hazel.

When we got to the sports ground—a pasture which had been coaxed into existence on the bog, so the ground was as springy as an innerspring mattress—Maria made me stop some distance from the entrance gate.

"We'll get out here," she said.

"But they're selling the tickets up there," I replied.

"That's why we will get out here," said Maria. I stopped the car, the back doors burst open, and the swarm of children spilled out. Maria, a young lady of fourteen, looked demurely around, hitched up her skirts modestly, and slipped under the fence as quick as a trout. The others followed her like minnows, except for Tricia and Kevin, whom I have unfortunately reared on the principle that they must pay money for anything they intend to purchase.

"Come on," said Maria, signaling to us.

58

I weighed my sole remaining pound against my principles, and I regret to say that my principles won out. I ignored Maria, Josephine, Jackie, Noel, Paddy and the other two stowaways who had slipped under the fence, and marched up to the admission gate.

"How much for children?" I asked.

"Children is it?" asked a man on whose face could be read much of the two-hundred-year history of Guinness' stout. "Why, I haven't sold a ticket for children all day." (The field behind him was swarming with children.) "Couldn't you just have them go down the road a bit and get under the fence and not be vexing me with the question?"

"Scram," I said to Kevin and Tricia, and gave the man my pound. He returned me eighteen shillings. "Tis a shilling for yourself, sir," he said, "and a shilling for the advice, so ye'll know better next time." So in I went.

I now discovered why Kevin was so keen on getting to the sports meeting. We had hardly arrived on the field before the contestants for the hundred-yard open were asked to kindly align themselves and give their names to the parish priest who was acting as chief steward. And there was Kevin, a nine-year-old pigmy among the six-footers, eagerly giving his name.

"You mean that you're going to run in this race?" I asked.

"There's a pound for first prize," said Kevin, "and I'm the best runner in North School."

Maybe he was. But the rest of the entrants were grown men with big frames and legs as knotted as blackthorn roots. The best runner in North School, Hermosa Beach, couldn't show his heels to these stalwarts. Kevin got away to a good start, his little legs whirling like a rabbit, and he had a fair chance of placing (two shillings and sixpence) when suddenly someone jumped clean over him from behind, and

59

Kevin promptly fell into a boghole. When he got out, the race was over.

"I was just getting going," said Kevin. "I'll do better in the next."

I bought him an ice cream. I might remark here it was what is called in Ireland a "soft" day. That is to say, there was a twenty-mile-an-hour wind slicing out of the west and panicking the dandelions and wild marigolds with which the sports arena was dotted. A fine rain came with the wind and the temperature was not much above forty degrees. The spectators were standing around shivering and eating ice cream, which was held in blue hands and applied to blue lips.

The next event was a four-hundred-forty-yard "dash," which Kevin said was just about his length. He got off ahead of the field and disappeared in a forest of pounding legs and flying feet, to reappear—in the rear. I think he would have done better except for the head wind, for I noticed that when he left the ground to leap through the air, he was slowed down in mid-flight by the raging westerly.

"That will be enough of that, son," I said when he was through. "In my youth I studied palmistry, and I fancy that until your mother gets back from wherever she is and sends us some money, I can join a group of tinkers and make enough for us to live on, telling fortunes."

I took him off and bought him another ice cream, leaving me with seventeen shillings. Jackeen and Noel and Maria appeared, looking so cold it was plain they needed ice cream too, which is what the Irish use to warm themselves with on "soft" days. So I parted with another half crown. The next event was a wheelbarrow race, and Kevin pleaded with me to be allowed to enter with Jackeen. I had never known grown men to be much good at wheelbarrow races, which are normally entered and won by children, so I consented.

60

I believe the two-pound prize would have been ours except that I had forgotten about Jackeen's lifelong struggle to keep his trousers up. He was to be the wheelbarrow, and as Kevin took his legs he begged him not to have the trousers off him, explaining that his suspenders were not of the best and the buttons could be improved upon. Kevin promised, picked Jackeen up by the legs and got into place. The other contestants were all grown men, long past the time when they had trouble keeping their trousers up. I was on the point of asking the priest whether Kevin and Jackeen might not start a few yards ahead because of the handicap of Jackeen's pants, when the whistle blew and the race started.

That is to say, everybody else started, and Jackeen, too. But Kevin was left holding Jackeen's pants which had burst from their moorings in the excitement of the start. Jackeen was prepared to poke Kevin in the nose, thinking he had done it on purpose, but I intervened, got the pants back on him and suggested that Kevin be the wheelbarrow, since I knew his trousers were securely fastened.

Off they went again, and had made a little headway when Jackeen's pants came down again. They did not come all the way down. By dint of some pretty skillful hitching on the run, he managed to keep them about at calf level (they were short pants). The two of them struggle along, Kevin laughing fit to burst and Jackeen furious, hitching his pants all the while. They got to the halfway mark, where the rules of the contest demanded that they must change positions. Jackeen was to be the wheelbarrow and Kevin was to hold his legs.

"Here," said Kevin, inspired. "Why don't you wear my pants? They stay up pretty good." There was a short discussion, and I regret that while the exchange was being effected, the winner crossed the finish line and the race was over.

This was followed by more ice cream, the day having got colder, and a warning to Kevin that he had done enough for the day and was to enter no more events. For myself, I said I would retire to the car out of the wind and the rain, and invited Kevin to do the same. He said he wanted to watch the next race, and off I went. (Tricia had found a cozy nook for herself in the front of the van where the ice cream was sold. Here she not only kept warm but managed to get several free ice creams which she gave to other children as if she owned the van and all its contents.)

I stayed in the car through the long jump (I discovered that Kevin in the interests of the family finances had entered this, pitting a jump of four feet against the winning jump of eighteen feet, seven inches), and through the bicycle race, musical chairs and the high jump. Indeed I had made myself almost cozy enough to drop off to sleep, when I heard high-pitched squeals and cries of excitement. One voice cried out above this tumult, "Look at the little Yank."

I got out of the car and made my way to the sports field. There was Kevin running around a circular track in the now familiar company of the six-foot men of Connemara.

"What event is this?" I asked a bystander.

"One mile open," was the reply. "The little Yank has done half a mile already."

"Kevin," I shouted as he came panting by me. "Get out of there."

"Arrah, leave him be," said the man. "It would be a delight if he won."

He didn't win. He was lapped a couple of times but he kept going and was two laps behind when the race was over. But when I got hold of him he wasn't the least bit downhearted.

"I'm still the fastest runner in North School," he said. "But I'm sorry I didn't get a prize."

I took him over to the car—he refused another ice cream—and thought for a little while.

"Kevin," I said, "how would you like to have a car?" He was still panting from having run three-quarters of a mile.

"A real car?" he asked.

"Yes," I replied. "This one. For running all those races."

"Gee," he said.

I had not filled out the registration papers, but did so there and then, entering the name of the owner as Kevin Myles Wibberley. Then I gave them to him.

The next day money came flooding in from America, and Kevin and Pegleg and I could relax.

SOME EXCELLENT GHOSTS

7. I AM a circumstantial believer in ghosts. That is to say, the circumstances about me at any particular time affect my belief in ghosts. In broad daylight, in the company of my friends, with all the clutter of the twentieth century about me, I do not believe in ghosts. If, in such circustances, one were to walk into my house with his head tucked under his arm, I would invite him to sit down, put his head on the table and have a cup of tea.

However, at night, in the vicinity of an old house with the wind whistling through the glassless windows and howling around the chimney pots, and the bare branches of trees clicking to each other and reaching out for me, I'm scared out of all reason of ghosts. The first ghost I met in Ireland was encountered in such circumstances—on the road over the bog to Clifden. It is a winding and unpaved road, plunging up and down little hills with boglands on both sides, and a mournful trickle of water to be heard at all times. The wind has a clean sweep on that road, howling in off the Atlantic, or sometimes, if the weather is fine, coming in over the top of the Twelve Pins in whose gaunt valleys men have been rumored to turn into stones, or withered trees, and stones have been known to go lumbering down to a stream, take a drink and then go lumbering back up the mountain again.

Anyway, on our first visit to Ireland, I had elected to drive Hazel over this bog in the long summer twilight. There were a lot of sheep about, but their eyes, shining in the dwindling light of the day, took on a satanic look and they shook their heads as if to warn us to go back. We got to a certain part of the road where it tops a hill between two rocks and then plunges down to the bottom of a little valley from which the light, at that hour, was excluded. I had just been telling Hazel about the stones that take a drink of water on All Saints Day once every hundred years, when she suggested that we ought to turn back.

"Why?" I asked.

"I don't like it here," said Hazel. "It's scary."

"But my dear girl," I said, "reflect that this is the twentieth century and you a product of an American university. No Americans have ever been touched by an Irish ghost, as a result of an agreement with the tourist board."

"Turn around and go back," said Hazel. "I think there's someone peering over the top of that rock at us."

"What's he look like?" I asked.

"He has a head like a codfish and smells awful," said Hazel. So I turned around.

Or rather I attempted to turn around. The road was extremely narrow and I did not want to get the wheels of the car stuck in the soft bog, for I knew we would be there all night. I didn't fancy spending the night in the company of something that looked like a large codfish and was peering over the top of the rock at my wife.

I estimate that it would have taken four locks backward and forward to have turned the car in the narrow road. But

I never made them. I drove forward, cut the wheels and put the car in reverse. It stayed in reverse. No matter how hard I tried, I could not get the wretched gear out of reverse. And there was that codfish thing looking at us over the rock. I fancied I could see it myself.

"The gear's stuck," I said. "We'll have to reverse all the way back to the village. But first you'll have to push me forward so I can straighten out on the road."

"I refuse to get out of this car," said Hazel.

"Don't be ridiculous," I said.

"You get out," said Hazel.

"My dear," I replied, "if there is any kind of a spirit around here with evil intentions, consider which of the two of us should be its victim. Should it be you, who I must admit are necessary to the welfare of our five children? Or should it be me, who am the breadwinner of the whole family, without whom they would all be on relief?"

Hazel got out of the car and pushed it forward, for she is a brave and sensible girl, and we reversed eight miles down the road to the outskirts of the village. There I wrestled the gearshift into neutral and found that thereafter I could get it into no gear at all. We left the car on the side of the road and walked the rest of the way home.

The following year, when I returned to Ireland without Hazel, I was driving in daylight over the same road with Tom's wife. When we got to the particular spot where the car had failed us, she said, "This is a terrible place for cars and motorbikes at nighttime."

"Oh?" I said.

"Yes, indeed," she said. "It is a haunted spot. My brother-in-law, God rest his soul, would not come by here on his motorcycle after sunset. He worked in Clifden and went eight miles out of his way rather than pass this particular place."

"What's it haunted by?" I asked.

"It is a thing with a head like a big fish that appears over the tops of those rocks there. It has some kind of a power over motorcycles and motorcars, for it always causes them to break down at this part of the road which it inhabits."

"Did your brother-in-law have engine trouble here after dark?" I asked.

"Twice he did," she said. "And ran home and left his motorcycle. And there's a lot of other people had the same trouble. You won't find many that will drive past here at nighttime."

"Did anything happen to any of the people whose cars broke down here?" I asked.

"Not that I know of," she said. "You're all right if you don't start fiddling with the engine. But if you're bending over with your head down in the hood so you can't see what's coming—then God help you."

"Snapped up like a fly?" I asked, and she nodded. Although it was daylight, I shuddered.

What interests me about ghosts in Ireland is that they tend to specialize. The fish-ghost on the bogs specialized in motorists or motorcyclists, snapping them up like Mayflies as soon as they started tinkering with their engines, which he used as bait. And there is a ghost in Killron that specialized in doctors. This particular ghost couldn't tolerate a doctor at all, and so haunted the house in the village which was normally assigned to the resident physician.

The visitations were not particularly spectacular—nothing more than the sounds of movement at night and the usual groans and slamming of doors. Occasionally all the lights in

68

the house would turn on of themselves or turn off according to the fancy of the ghost. But there were no bloody footprints left upon the floors, nor any headless horrors ascending the staircase with a candle held in one skeleton hand.

On the other hand, this somewhat modest ghost got rid of three doctors.

The first died suddenly in the house, but since the medical diagnosis gave the cause of death as spinal meningitis, no particular significance was attached to the event. His successor, occupying the same house, went out of his mind in a very short time and had to be put in a mental home, or so I am told. The third doctor, appointed to the village by the government health service, was a young man who, when the lights went on and off in the house mysteriously, looked for a short in the electrical circuits rather than reach for a bell, book and candle. He paid for it, however, for he was found as dead as a doornail staring up at the ceiling, with all the lights in the house on—or so I was told.

Thereafter, the house was sold to someone who was not a doctor, and who has flourished in the place. A new house was built for the village doctors and nothing has happened to any of them in it.

A few years ago there was another visitation on the bog which was seen by many of the villagers. It consisted of a tiny white light, no bigger than the light of a bicycle seen from some distance away. Many who saw it thought it was a cyclist riding along the bog road. But as time went by, this light came down the road toward the watchers, waxing in size until it was quite as big and bright as an automobile headlight. It never did anybody any harm. Several say it passed right by them and they felt no fear nor any heat from it. It was, of course, the fairy light, and a man has no need to fear the fairies if he has done nothing to annoy them.

In another village there was a poltergeist. A man was passing by the barroom of a small inn and noticed smoke coming from beneath the door. Suspecting that the place was afire, he tried to open the door, but it was locked. He went for help, and having got two or three to batter the door down, they found the door had been opened from the inside. There was a considerable fire raging in the barroom but it had not reached the door. They formed a bucket brigade and got the fire out, and were just congratulating themselves when it flared up again. The spot was remarkable, for the flames appeared in a corner on the ceiling.

They threw buckets of water up at the corner and got the flames out, but they had hardly done so before another fire broke out in an opposite corner of the room—again on the ceiling.

By the time this little blaze was under control, there was a general suspicion that the barroom had been taken over by a poltergeist, or mischievous ghost.

There were several other fires in the same barroom and all of them started in the oddest places—under the floors, behind cupboards, and so on. The oddest and last of them started in the old wooden counter which served as a bar. The fire started in the center of a plank four inches thick and normally sodden with Guinness to which might be added a modicum of whisky on a Saturday night. Anyway, it was a good thick damp plank, and the fire started in the middle of it and to the amazement of the customers, burned outward toward the surface.

That was enough. The priest was summoned, and he came to the conclusion that a poltergeist was haunting the place. Poltergeists are usually in the company of a human familiar, and the priest suspected that one of two girls serving in the barroom was the familiar in question. She was found a job in another village and thereafter the fires ceased and there has been no recurrence.

The best ghost story I picked up about Ireland concerned Maynooth, the seminary not far from Dublin where young men are trained for the priesthood. According to the story, a young student, noted for his piety, was found hanging from the window of his room one morning. Some thought it was a case of suicide while of unsound mind and others speculated that in the middle of the night he had been seized by the devil, who had put a rope around his neck and flung him out the window. Not long after, another student was reported to have hanged himself in the same room and it was now strongly suspected that an evil presence had taken up its abode in this particular room and would destroy any who spent the night there—driving them to suicide to be sure of obtaining possession of their immortal souls.

A young priest then decided he would spend the night in the room and wrestle with this demon. He was given permission to do so, and having gone to confession to cleanse his soul of all sin and be in a perfect state of grace, he entered the room and the door was locked.

During the night there were sounds of struggle in the room —sounds like a man's body being hurled around—and cries of agony and of despair. But though the door was tried several times, it was impossible either to open it or batter it down. When dawn came and the first cock crowed, the door opened quietly and the priest came out.

But it was not the same priest who had gone in. The man who had entered the room had been a vigorous, curly-haired fellow, well-muscled, erect, an excellent hurley player. The man who came out was in the last tatters of old age.

71

His cheeks were sunken, his hair thin and white. His hands trembled and his eyelids were red with years and devoid of lashes.

All he could tell his companions was the room must be sealed so no one could enter it again. This was done, a shrine being erected in front of the door.

I am much attached to this particular ghost story, and regret only that it is not true. The facts are that a young student did commit suicide in a room at Maynooth over a hundred years ago. But no devil occupied the place, destroying others who spent the night there. In fact, nothing in particular happened at all, which is a great pity.

THE WILLING HEART

8. I HAD hired a little Ford Anglia which we had named Peanut, upon arrival in Ireland, and it proved to be the most expensive automobile ever to come into my possession. It was not the gasoline consumption that put it in the luxury bracket. It did an honest thirty-five miles to the gallon, and driving it was somewhat like driving a roller skate down the road.

No, the car was economical on fuel. But the hire charge was a murderous fifty-one dollars a week. This is the minimum price for which the smallest of cars may be hired in Ireland in midsummer, and I suppose the price must be based on the rooted Irish belief that the sidewalks of New York are paved with gold. This is largely the fault of returning Irish-Americans, who act as though they are.

I decided at the end of two weeks to turn in Peanut, and out of the money budgeted for automobile expenses buy a second-hand car in Dublin. I have a fair amount of experience in the purchase of second-hand cars, but my experience is American. The man who deals in second-hand cars in Ireland, I thought, was very likely a horse dealer in his youth

73

and served an apprenticeship in filling teeth and polishing hooves to make a broken-down dray horse look like a hunter. Suspecting this, whether rightly or not, I decided I'd best take Michael John along with me.

Michael John I had met the year before in Ireland. He runs a butcher's shop in the village of Kinvara and also a radio shop, a bicycle store, possesses the only cold storage facilities in the village, builds houses, helps organize the annual carnival and is very fond of my children. Michael John drives the sick to the hospital, the groom to the church and the intoxicated to their homes.

Anyway, I called in at Kinvara with Kevin and Patricia to see Michael John, and told him I was going to Dublin to turn in Peanut and buy another car. He looked at me with compassion and shook his head.

"They'll take the gold out of your teeth," he said, "and sell you a wheelbarrow."

"Pity you can't come," said I.

"A pity indeed."

"You have, I know, a new house to build."

"I have."

"And you must start on it immediately."

"I must."

"Well," I said, "I'll let you know how I get on."

"Wait a minute," said Michael John. "I'd never rest easy if I let you go alone. I'll get my pajamas and a toothbrush and go with you."

"What about the house?" I asked.

"I'll start tomorrow," said Michael John.

It takes about three and a half hours for a man of my age to drive from Galway to Dublin. The distance is only one hundred thirty miles and the road is excellent. But I am no hand at driving through flocks of sheep, herds of cattle and

74

clutches of ducks and geese, all of which frequent the roads of Ireland. Some are being driven to or from the market. Some are being driven to or from the pasture. Others are there, in my view, because there is a sporting chance they'll get hit by a car and return a quick profit to the owner. We went through perhaps a hundred thousand head of cattle, and perhaps five or six times that many sheep, and at the other end of these flocks, there was Dublin, dirty and cheerful as ever, with the lovely white swans gliding among the shiploads of Guinness on the river. I proposed that we stay at the Gresham, but Michael John was horrified.

"Sure, nobody but rich people stay there," he said. "We wouldn't want to be seen mixing with them. We'll stay at the Belvedere."

We went round to the Belvedere, but the Belvedere was full. So was Grant's and so were the next six hotels we tried. I asked the clerk at one hotel why the city was so crowded.

"Tis the Battle of the Boyne," he replied.

"The Battle of the Boyne?" I repeated.

"Yes. All the Orangemen are down here from Belfast, celebrating the great and glorious day when they licked the tar out of us Irish a couple of hundred years ago. And they've a great thirst on them, thanks be to God."

Without going too deeply into Irish history, the situation was roughly the equivalent of the Daughters of the American Revolution booking every hotel in London solid to celebrate the surrender of Cornwallis at Yorktown.

Eventually we stayed in a boarding house, where I believe we got the last room available in Dublin.

The next morning, after an abundant breakfast of bacon, and eggs, and sausages, and orange juice, and soda bread and tea, we went out to buy a car. I presumed that we would

75

go to a second-hand car dealer or at least to an automobile agency. We went to a garage.

Before we went in, Michael John looked at my shirt and his own and shook his head. "They're too clean," he said. "They'll double the price on us."

Inside the garage a mechanic in clothes obtained from a ragbag was leaning, as in prayer, over a Chevrolet which had obviously run its last mile.

"Have you an old car for sale?" asked Michael John.

"I have," said the mechanic, eyeing the Chevrolet, and mildly surprised. I surmised that prayer should be answered so soon.

"Would you like my opinion on that car?" asked Michael John.

"I would," said the mechanic.

"Twould be wonderful for keeping the rain off the hens," answered Michael John.

"Oh, this isn't the car I had in mind at all," said the mechanic, "though you misjudge her. She looks bad, I know, but she has a engine that would surprise you. Tis that Hudson over there. She was running around the city as a hackney until three weeks ago."

"Was it the police that made you take her off the road?" asked Michael John, and walked thoughtfully over to the Hudson.

The car had the appearance of a wreck which had been straightened by an unskilled man using a sledge hammer. It was covered with a black substance which was sticky and smelled of tar. I opened the front door and inspected the speedometer. It gave the mileage as 98,000, which was probably the second time around for the gauge—so the true mileage was at least 198,000. I developed an immediate and idiotic affection for the car.

76

"How much?" I asked.

"Twenty pounds," said the mechanic. He seemed to be holding his breath.

"Will it run?" I asked.

"Run?" said he. "Why, we'd enter it in the Galway Plate if it wasn't for the water jump."

"I suppose it will do all of five miles to the gallon," I said.

"Five miles to the gallon?" echoed the mechanic to Dublin at large. "Lord save us, how do you suppose we could use it as a hackney around the city at a profit at five miles to the gallon?"

Michael John detached one of the parking lights with

77

a gentle blow of his hand and threw it into a box of junk on the floor.

"The upholstery is fit for a Lord Mayor," said the mechanic, retrieving the parking light and putting it back in place without a blush. "And if you had her out on the highway and gave her her head, she'd do twenty-eight."

"If ye got her out on the highway at all, it would be a miracle," said Michael John.

"Will she start?" I asked.

"She's no battery in her," said the mechanic. "I'll get one and start her and ye'll be delighted with the sound of the engine. Are those your two little children now?"

"They are," I replied, looking at Kevin and Patricia, who had wandered into the garage.

"Aren't they the grandest little children I ever saw," he said, clucking like an overfond matron.

"Is this the car you're going to buy, Daddy?" asked Kevin, who is achingly devoid of any subtlety.

"No," said Michael John grimly, "Not if I have to strangle him."

The mechanic went off and returned with a battery. He also had with him the proprietor of the garage, who was doing his best to conceal his incredulity.

"I'll be sorry to part with her," said the proprietor. "She's a grand old car to this day."

"Yes," said Michael John, "tis like burying your grandmother. You know she'd go someday but tis always a surprise." He turned to the mechanic. "Never mind with the battery," he said, "we'll look somewhere else."

"I don't mind cutting the price a little," said the proprietor. "I need the floor space."

"You do that," said Michael John, looking around at the undergrowth of oil-smeared second-hand autmobile parts

78

that littered the floor. "You do that, indeed." He led me firmly outside and back to Peanut.

We now drove around through back streets where soot, damp, wind, dust, tattered papers, broken cardboard boxes, tottering houses, railroad tracks, cobblestones and noisome refuse made as wretched a slum area as I have ever seen. In this jungle of shattering poverty, only the children were cheerful. Underpriviledged, undernourished and under-clothed they might be. But they were as merry as sparrows in a field of wheat, and played with balls made of brown paper rolled up and tied with string and wet with gutter water.

Through these crumbling streets lined by crumbling houses we drove until we came to an alley, and down the bottom of the alley found a building which was a surprise in that it was standing up when it should be falling down. The interior was dark and the greasy ganglia of automobiles were strewn about, like offal in a shambles. A man was lying under the chassis of a car, cutting it in half with an acetylene torch. Michael John summoned him upright by kicking the sole of his foot. The man came out and looked us over in wonderment.

"I'm looking for a car—cheap," said Michael John.

"How cheap?" asked the man.

"Twenty pounds," said Michael John.

The man shook his head. "When they get down to twenty pounds," he said, "they're more valuable as scrap."

"Cash," said Michael John. The man shook his head in deep sorrow.

"I just cut one up that might have done you," he said. "Haven't a thing. You wouldn't go for an old motorbike now? There's a twin-port Norton over there—1925. Very good. Little hard to start, but a good runner."

79

I had visions of the four of us on the motorcycle braving the ocean of sheep and cattle, ducks, geese and donkeys which separates Dublin from Galway.

"No," said Michael John, "I'll try somewhere else."

"I'll give you a friendly word," said the man, relighting his electric torch. "When they see you coming they'll charge you double."

"That's the truth of it," said Michael John, eyeing his clean shirt again.

"Well, good luck," said the man, and returned to the task of cutting the car in two. We tried several more junk yards, but the best offer was a five-ton truck. The door fell off when I opened it. I had now come to the conclusion that Dublin is the final resting place of all the beaten-up, exhausted and dead automobiles in the world. Michael John finally agreed with some reluctance that we should try a used-car dealer. He was unwilling to do so as it seemed to be against both his principles and his best instincts.

We found one, again in a grimier part of Dublin. There was a fish barrow outside surrounded by tattered women. On the barrow were the remains of a small ray, butchered, bloodied and far from fresh. We found a salesman and he smiled brightly at us.

"I have just what you want," he said. "Nice little Morris 10. Runs very well. Good upholstery . . ."

"And you'll be sorry to part with it," said Michael John.

"Divil a bit of it," said the salesman. "I've been trying to get rid of it for weeks."

This astounding honesty produced a rapport between the two immediately. We went to look at the car. It was carefully placed in the gloomier part of the garage, so all I could see immediately was that there was something resembling a small automobile there. It had a heavy list to starboard forward, accounted for by the fact that the right front tire was flat.

"Will it start?" asked Michael John.

"I'll put it this way," said the salesman. "Sometimes it will and sometimes it won't. Tis like the rocket program at Cape Canaveral. Even the experts don't know."

"It will start," said a mechanic, emerging from the gloom.

He turned on the ignition and pulled a piece of baling wire that protruded from the dashboard. The little Morris shuddered and roared into life. Kevin had been standing behind the car with Tricia, and they disappeared in a bank of dense blue smoke coming from the exhaust.

"She'll do thirty to the gallon," said the salesman.

"Of what—oil?" asked Michael John, eyeing the smoke cloud from which Kevin was beginning to emerge.

"I see that you're a cynic," said the salesman. "She has had a ring job—within living memory," he added, looking towards Heaven for forgiveness.

The mechanic switched off the engine and we all coughed a little. The salesman suggested with great daring that we drive her around the block. The flat tire was replaced, and we climbed in and trickled out of the garage. It soon developed that she was slow on her helm. A turn of the steering wheel to the right or the left produced no immediate effect. Several seconds later, however, the car would swerve abruptly in the direction desired like a sheep with the staggers.

The brakes worked but jerked the car crazily to the left or right—it was impossible to anticipate which. The clutch seemed good—I fancied she had no clutch lining but was operating on the rivets. The gearbox was sound and I could detect no knock from the crankshaft bearings. The oil pressure was nil, but that might have been because the gauge wasn't working.

We drove back to the garage and climbed out. "How much?" asked Michael John.

"Sixty pounds," said the salesman.

"I'll give you forty," I said, in spite of myself.

The salesman and Michael John exchanged looks of astonishment. The salesman looked a little disappointed, as if he had achieved a victory so easy that it was without savor. Michael John excused himself, led me out of the garage, and stood me by the barrow on which reposed the frightful remains of the ray.

"This gentleman," he said to the fishmonger, "is writing a book about Ireland, God help him, and would be interested in anything you can tell him about the fish business."

"Fivepence," said the fishmonger, wrapping up the ray's remnants and handing them to me. I paid him and returned to the garage, chastened.

Michael John and the salesman were in a huddle. I stood back and explained to Tricia that we were not going to have fish for dinner but I had been tricked into buying a piece of fish I didn't want and I had no means of disposing of it.

"Give it to me," said Tricia and I did so. She went away and returned without the fish but with two ice creams, one of which she gave to Kevin.

"What did you do with the fish?" I asked.

"I traded it to a man for two ice creams," she said. I thought this over and sent her down to help Michael John.

There now followed a great deal of bargaining between him and the salesman. Since I had been expelled to the edges of the arena as unworthy of the conflict, I caught but a snatch of what was going on. I pieced together the following:

"Will you put four new tires on her?"

"I will not. I have a large family and have to limit my public charities."

"She'll never get out of Dublin with the tires she has."

"I can see you're a pessimist. She would make Maynooth easy."

"That's a hundred and twenty miles from Galway."

"I can give you a retread on the one with the blister on it."

"Will you look at those two rear tires for the love of God. They'd wring tears from a heathen."

"It was my wife who told me not to come to work this morning," said the salesman. "She had a dream last night that I'd fall in with thieves and they'd take my last copper."

"I suppose that you'll buy her a nice bit of jewelry with the profit you're making out of the old car," said Michael John. "Or perhaps you'll treat her to a weekend in London."

So it went on while I stood fretfully in the background and Kevin and Tricia ate their ice cream and managed somehow to get a considerable amount of gearbox oil on themselves. Finally Michael John came to me gloomily.

"We can have her for forty-five pounds," he said. "He'll put two new tires on the rear and two retreads on the front." I made a quick calculation and discovered that discounting the tires we were getting the car for twenty-seven pounds. I was delighted, but Michael John was determined to pay no more than forty.

He made a last valiant effort, when it came to paying.

"Give him forty pounds," he hissed to me. "Count them out in fives, one by one. The sight of the money may soften his heart."

I did so, counting out the five-pound notes until I came to forty, and then I stopped.

"Forty-five," said the salesman.

"Forty," said Michael John.

"Forty-five."

I added the additional five-pound note, but Michael John had not done yet. We climbed into the car and he backed her up to the gas pump. "Fill her up," he said.

The salesman looked at him in pure admiration. "By God, you're a man after my own heart," he said, and the two of them shook hands.

With a tankful of free gasoline, which brought the price of the car down to forty pounds, we took off for Galway.

Just past Maynooth one of the tires blew out.

"They're all sharks in Dublin," said Michael John as we mounted the spare.

But the little Morris performed so well on the long haul from Dublin to Galway that we decided we should call her The Willing Heart.

FOLK MEDICINE

9. TOM was the source of the greater part of my information in Killron, and one day we were discussing ailments of different kinds and the advances of modern medicine and Tom told me that modern medicine may be good but it was not as effective as the old medicine in some cases.

"I have known of men who have had a *cleddin* and the doctors could do nothing for them but they have been cured by a folk doctor, if you know what I mean," he said.

"What's a *cleddin?*" I asked.

"Well it's a disarrangement of the bones, do you see, in your chest. When a man does a lot of stooping work like rowing and footing the turf he is likely to get a *cleddin* after some time. And if it is not cured, he will waste away and die."

"Surely such a condition could be diagnosed by X ray and corrected," I said.

"Why, so it could," said Tom. "But I have still known men who had a *cleddin* and were laid up in bed with it for years and their lives despaired of, and then they were cured by a folk doctor."

"What does the folk doctor do?" I asked.

"Well, he straightens the man out, which is the most important thing," said Tom. "He will stand behind the man, do you see, on a block of wood, and dig his hands into his chest underneath his ribs. Then he will lift him up off the ground by his ribs, pulling him back against himself so that the whole weight of the man is on his ribs that the doctor has his fingers hooked underneath. It is a pretty painful thing, I haven't a doubt. But it works.

"Then when he has done this, which is the first part of the straightening out, he puts the man on the floor and tramples on his spine. I won't say that he tramples, exactly. He knows where to put his foot, do you see. And he puts his foot there and brings his weight down on the spot and you can hear the bones crack and adjust themselves until they are straight again.

"Then he has the man go home and rest up and not do any work for a while but use suckage on himself."

"And what is suckage?" I asked.

"Well, you take an empty tumbler and put it on your stomach a few inches from your navel and leave it there for a while. And if you have been sick with a *cleddin,* the glass will suck your skin and flesh up inside of itself. I've seen it done, so I know that it works. You do this every day, and after a while the glass will no longer suck the skin up inside of itself, and that shows that the cleddin is leaving you."

This suckage, I suppose, is an Irish variety of cupping—a medieval form of medicine supposed to draw poisons out of the body.

I was surprised that there was still some belief in folk

medicine in Ireland; and although Tom did not himself place much faith in it, yet he had heard a great deal about it and was willing to talk on the subject. It appears that folk doctors not only tend men but animals as well. They have to operate secretly, of course, and people nowadays go to them only when they think that the college-trained doctor is doing them no good.

Sometimes, Tom said, it happens that a horse spends a night out on the bogs in the rain and cold—straying from its normal pasturage and getting lost in the dark. After such an experience the horse will develop "haws." The symptoms are that it walks with its hind legs far apart, and develops a little wart on the lid of its eye. The veterinarian can cure this condition, but his bills are high and his cure is tedious. The folk doctor can do it much faster and cheaper.

The procedure is to cut the wart out of the animal's eyelid. This is easier said than done. It is a painful process and the animal is very scared. One man takes the horse by the lower lip and another by the upper lip. Held in this manner, the horse is in such discomfort that he will not jerk his head. Then the doctor takes a needle and thread and sews the affected eyelids together so he can operate on them more easily. He then cuts out the "haw" or wart. As soon as the horse is released, he is over his attack, and you may harness him there and then or ride him off and he will be as good as ever he was.

There is also a procedure for resetting dislocated shoulder joints on horses. The vet, I am told, immobilizes the whole limb, and it takes several weeks for the joint to mend. But the folk doctor makes a cut over the place where the joint is dislocated. He makes a second cut above this and another below it. He then inserts a stick which is threaded in some manner through these cuts. The animal is then released with such bandages as are needed to stanch the bleeding. In no time at all, the joint will have healed and the stick may be taken out.

Veterinarians, Tom said, do not believe in this method of mending dislocations of the bones in animals. But it has worked in many cases.

The treatment is, to say the least of it, rough, but the Irish have not the sentiment about animals that the English possess. It would be wrong to say they are needlessly cruel to them. But they do not dote on them and fondle them as the English do. They treat them as a lesser order of creation which is not entitled to the same consideration as a human being.

"God bless all in this house, except of course the dog and the cat," is an Irish greeting on entering someone's home. It is proper to except the household animals, for they have no souls, and it is hardly right to call down God's blessing on a creature which is soulless. Yet I have heard a man exclaim on taking a sup of milk on a hot day, "God's blessing on the cow," so in this kind of blessing (for benefits received) there is no sacrilege involved.

Donkeys are now declining in use as beasts of burden in Ireland. At one time they were widely employed, and a tiny ass drawing a laden cart was a familiar sight on Irish roads. Now, though some still use donkey carts, and others use donkeys to bring the turf out of the bog in baskets if there is no good road handy, donkeys are largely unemployed. As a result, you will see, particularly in Connemara, many donkeys on the road whose hooves have grown into crippling arcs on which they can scarcely stand and only shuffle about to get food. If the donkey were of any use to its owner, he would certainly pare the hooves and shoe the donkey. But the animal is useless and so its hooves are allowed to grow, and it walks around in misery on the overgrown hooves, finding it harder and harder to forage for grass or get out of the way of automobiles. Such a thing would bring a huge public outcry in England or America, and the owner of the donkey would be fined heavily and, indeed, might be jailed.

When at one time I was considering bringing a dog to Ireland, I consulted the Irish consulate and he advised me to take it to England to be kenneled for the required period of six months.

"You know how it is with the English," he said. "They have more affinity with animals, as it were, than we." And so they have. I do not mean this as a criticism, but only that the Englishman extends human qualities and human feelings to animals and the Irishman does not. Maybe tenderness towards animals comes only with public prosperity. Prosperous nations such as Britain and the United States are humane. But a hundred years ago, when farmers were less financially secure—when the word poverty had not been softened to underprivileged—people were not humane to animals at all. In the poorer nations, Spain, Portugal, and among the French peasantry and in Ireland, animals are often neglected if there is no use for them. It is not cruelty, so much as the harsh necessity of looking after oneself.

But I have not yet done with folk medicine.

For many years I have suffered from a peculiar condition which has at times been diagnosed as a faulty heart, and at others as a shortage of sugar in the blood. The symptoms consist of the onset of a terrible hunger—so fierce that I tremble and must immediately stuff myself with any kind of food (preferably sweet stuffs) on which I can lay my hands.

One day, seated at a table for a huge Irish tea, a young lady said that that very morning she had been walking down a boreen and had been unfortunate enough to be overtaken by the *firgorcha* (I give a phonetic spelling, but do not find the word in an Irish dictionary).

"*Firgorcha?*" I said. "What is that?"

"Well," she replied, "there is a certain kind of a plant or maybe it is a mineral or a little stone and if you tread on it, all the nourishment is drained out of your body and you start to tremble and perspire and are overcome by hunger. You will eat anything you can get at that moment, and if you do not eat, you will faint from starvation and perhaps die."

"I have had the *firgorcha* for years," I said. "Is there no cure for it?"

"Only that you must watch where you put your foot, and if you are attacked, have a little food handy."

"What kind of a plant or a mineral is it that does this?" I asked, but on this point the young lady could not satisfy me. It was a special plant or mineral, that was all.

Another time I came across a cure for whoopingcough, but it has a complicated background, stemming from something that happened long, long ago. At that time there was a certain poor widow who had neither a bit of land nor a cow of her own, and no means whatever to provide for her daughter, who was young and sickly. One day, going about a mountain side bemoaning her fate and picking up a few sticks to make a fire, she found herself in a beautiful little valley with a small lake and standing beside the lake a gleaming white cow. A fairy appeared and told her she might milk the cow and take it to her child, but she must never spill the milk on the ground. The widow thanked her, milked the cow, and brought the milk to her child, who drank it greedily and very soon began to get well.

A spiteful neighbor, seeing the child recovering so fast,

90

asked the widow what she was feeding it, and she said it was the milk of a fairy cow in the valley and she might have as much as she liked of it.

The neighbor, in her malice, went therefore early the following morning to the valley and found the white cow. She had no need of the milk herself, but she was determined the widow woman should not have any. So she milked the cow, squirting the milk on the ground, and hardly had the first drop hit the earth than cow, valley, lake and woman disappeared, to be replaced by seven beautiful streams whose waters were milk-white. When the widow woman came to get her milk, the cow was gone and she sat by one of the streams weeping and the stream, taking pity on her, said, "Take some of my water to your child and it will do just as well as the milk." She did so and the child waxed healthy on the water and indeed, the water from any one of the Seven Streams which are in County Clare is powerful medicine to this day.

However, there came a time when the woman was too old to go to the stream and the child not strong enough, and the child was taken with the *triuch* (whoopingcough).

Again the old widow was beside herself with woe, and wished the white cow would come to the door and give her child some milk and some ease. Then a fairy who was behind the pot over the fire said to her, "Stand by the road and ask the first man you see riding a white horse what you should give your child for the *triuch*, and whatever he says, give that to the child, and the *triuch* will go."

"Thank you very much," said the widow.

"It is a pleasure to help a decent body," said the fairy.

The widow stood by the road and, sure enough, a man came by on a white horse. She asked him what she should give her child who had the *triuch*, and the man said, "A little white snail and a pinch of salt." The woman gave this to the child and the child was cured.

"Well," I said to the lady who had told me this tale, "that is a pretty story, but I do not think that a white snail and a pinch of salt will cure the whoopingcough."

"I will not go that far with you, though I like to agree with people," said the lady. "There is a woman in this village whose child had the whoopingcough only a month ago. The child was losing weight and the doctors could do nothing for her. So the mother remembered what had happened to the old widow, and she stood three days by the road waiting for a man to come by on a white horse, but most of them came by on bicycles.

"Then on the third day BJ came by riding a white horse. You know BJ?"

"Michael John's brother?" I asked.

"The same. The woman stopped him and said, 'BJ, my child has the *triuch*. What should I give her for it?'

" 'How am I to know, ma'am?' asked BJ.

" 'Well, you must say something,' said the woman.

" 'But suppose I said something and it made the child sicker.'

" 'I don't care. You are to tell me what to give the child, and I know it will make it well.'

" 'Well, then,' said BJ, 'if that is the way of it, give it some honey and my blessing. Good day to you, ma'am.'

" 'Good day to you, BJ.' "

"Did the mother give the child some honey?" I asked.

"She did indeed, and after the first spoonful the child was easy and the *triuch* had gone. Tell me, how many boys were there in your father's family?"

"Seven. He was the youngest."

"And in your father's father's family?"

"I believe there were seven also."

"Then it is likely that you are the seventh son of a seventh son and would make a good doctor. I have been having a muscle spasm in my legs at night and it plagues me and I cannot get to sleep."

"A cup of tea between us will do it no harm," said I, and so we had the tea and some more enjoyable talk together.

VOYAGE IN A GLAUCÓG

10.   I HAD been planning for some time to go to Inishmor, the largest of the three islands of Aran off the Galway coast, and, at first, thought I would take the steamer which sails three or four times a week. Indeed, I went to the tourist office in Galway (which is called in Irish *Ofig Bord Failte*–Office of the Board of Welcome) to ask about the steamer, and whether one should make reservations to sail on it.

"You can't make reservations," said the girl. "You go down to the quay and line up with everyone else and hope that you'll get a ticket. That's the glory of it," she added, as if nothing would suit her better than to be caught in a multitude of anxious people, some with goats, and some with pigs and others with heifers, and some with children, and some with cameras and baskets of lunch and bananas which must not be squashed, and eggs, likewise, to fight it out to get a ticket on the steamer over to Aran.

But I did not particularly relish the idea of such glory, and I cast about for a better and more appropriate method of getting to the lonely and famous islands thirty miles off the Galway coast.

I consulted Tom as to whether there might be someone with a *glaucóg* (an Irish fishing smack, carrying jib, staysail and gaff-headed mainsail) who might take Kevin, Patricia and me over to Aran. He consulted with his brother Pat, and we made the matter the topic of an hour and a half's debate over glasses of black Guinness in the parlor of Finherty's bar.

Pat contrived to sit as much as he could behind the open door, so all I could see of him was a knobby hand clutching a pint of Guinness and a pair of legs clad in ill-used Donegal tweed trousers. This was because we were having our drink after closing hours, and the *Guarda* might object, though most of them are decent civilized men. His conversation came from behind the door in a ghostly manner. Tom, somewhat bolder, tore a page out of the *Irish Independent*, put it on the broken-down couch to sit on, nicely taking his place among the elite but at the same time acknowledging there were too many mackerel scales on his trousers to sit directly on the fabric of the couch. For myself, I selected a bentwood chair, using the remainder of the *Irish Independent* as a seat cover.

"There's Padraic MacNan over on Inishnee," I said, when all had taken a reverent sip of their Guinness and uttered an "A-r-r-h," which is the proper reaction.

"There is so," said Tom.

Pat said nothing and there ensued several minutes of silence. I was conscious that the ice around Padraic MacNan was a bit thin. On the other hand, since the silence seemed likely to last through the whole pint of Guinness, I plunged recklessly in again.

"Padraic MacNan has a *glaucóg*, I think," I said.

95

"He has so," said Tom.

Pat again said nothing, and we had another silence.

"It's a pretty good boat from what I could see of it," I continued, determined to force the issue.

The reaction to this was a choking sound from Pat behind the door.

Tom looked around slowly and severely at his brother, or rather in his direction—Pat being but partially visible.

"His is a good boat," said Tom. He paused and surveyed the room to see that no one had sneaked in unobserved, and then strained his head back over the couch to see who might be out in the corridor. "'Tis a good boat," he repeated, "but it's not the best."

"Not the best," said Pat.

That was it, then. No fisherman likes to criticize another fisherman's boat. That is the equivalent of criticizing another man's wife. On the other hand, there is a variation of qualities among boats, just as among wives, and that has to be taken into consideration. But I had indelicately forced Tom into making a statement on the qualities of Padraic MacNan's boat.

"She's not in top shape," said Tom, anxious to heal the wound before it was noticed. "She's not in top shape. I'll put it that way."

"There's the *Caper*," said Pat, from behind the door.

"There is," said Tom cheerfully and looked at me expectantly. Plainly it was all right for me to inquire about the *Caper*.

"Is she good?" I asked.

"The best," said Tom. "None better. She's eighty years old if she's a day."

"Eighty would be right," said Pat.

"I believe I could say ninety now, and not be far wrong," said Tom.

"Eighty," said Pat, from his ambush.

There followed a discussion touching on several drownings and casting-aways, while I debated whether I should trust myself and my two children on a sea voyage of some thirty miles to an eighty-year-old boat—or it might be a hundred, for that matter.

I inquired whether the *Caper* was still being used, and was assured she was in use almost daily, was the fastest *glaucóg* on the coast, and had taken several races. Her owner was the finest sailor in the whole of Galway, to which might be added County Clare and also County Mayo.

"Is she safe?" I inquired.

"Safer than the *Lusitania*," said Tom, mentioning the first big ship that came to his mind. On this dubious assurance we agreed that the following day we would go over to Carna and interview Joe, the owner of the *Caper,* to see whether he would take us over to Aran.

We found Joe in a field of his farm, turning the hay. It was a tiny field, surrounded by stone walls, and so full of boulders I believe the hay must have been cut with scissors, for it seemed impossible to swing a scythe in such a field. (Those who talk about mechanizing Irish farming have never seen the fields of Connemara.)

Joe spotted us immediately, put down his rake, came over the stone wall dividing his field from the road and seated himself in the ditch. We did likewise—Tom and I—and Joe, having selected a long stem of grass, put it in his mouth and I followed suit. We chewed together for a while, not looking at each other but at the stone wall and the ditch, nonetheless getting some kind of feeling of each other.

Joe was a man in his mid-fifties, white-haired, thin-faced,

blue-eyed and boldly handsome despite his years. He had no sooner seated himself in the ditch than a swarm of children, seeing their father was not working, gathered around him. He looked like an old sheep dog among its puppies, and had the kindness and wisdom that went with the part.

There were three little girls—smiling and very shy, yet flirtatious. They would peek at me now and then when they thought I was not looking. When I caught them at it, they giggled and nudged one another and looked away and blushed. There were three older boys—the eldest about eleven. They were shy also and they smiled, too, but they had forgotten how to blush. They were curly-headed, wore short pants and sea boots, and looked more like miniature men than boys.

None of these children could speak any English. I inquired their names and was met only with giggles and blushes.

"The little ones have no English," said Joe. "They haven't been to school yet."

"Do the boys speak English?" I asked.

"A little," he said. "They don't learn much in school. It's all Irish. That's foolish, too," he continued. "For every one of them must emigrate. There's no living for them here. They must go off to America and earn what they can, and it's little good talking Irish will do for them there." He looked solemnly at his three sons whom one day he would send off down the road to Galway or Cork to catch the boat to America and perhaps never see again. They returned his look steadily. That was what lay ahead of them. It was what lay ahead of most of the Irish; it was what God had planned, and He would look after them all.

"Were you ever in America yourself?" I asked. I could not believe that so simple and childlike a man could ever have been there. Here, I thought, was one Irishman whose whole life had been spent in this Irish-speaking part, among his little fields and with his fishing smack. He would know nothing of a city bigger perhaps than Galway, and might have been there but two or three times in his life.

"I was," said Joe with a gentle smile. "Chicago."

Chicago! That roaring, bustling, feisty city with its machine politics and its gangland background, its stockyards and railroad complex, and its tough, ruthless tenderloin district. How could this simple Irish-speaking fisherman ever have survived in Chicago?

"I was there in 1929 and 1930 and I came back in 1931. There was no work," he said.

"What did you do?" I asked.

"I worked in a factory for six months. Making Majestic radios. Then the factory closed down. After that I did odd jobs until I'd saved my fare home."

"You had a bad time," I said.

"I was young," he replied, and looked at his three sons.

"Would you go back again?" I asked.

"I would not," he said simply.

"But you will send your sons?"

"They will have to go. There is no work for them here. No living to be made."

"But times may have changed when they have grown up."

"Times will not change in Ireland," he said with conviction.

We turned now to the question of hiring his boat to take me to the Aran Islands. But we could not come directly to this point. Ancient Irish courtesy frowns on such directness and so we talked first about sailing and different kinds of sailing vessels.

There are roughly three kinds in Ireland—the nobbie or hooker, which might be described as a big ketch (two-masted, with a fore- and mainsail, and carrying before the

99

foremast a staysail and jib). Then there is the *glaucóg* (I give a phonetic spelling), which is a cutter, and the *pucan,* which is a sloop.

All are fast disappearing. Working sail is going all over the world, and sailing as an art continues now in the form of pleasure craft.

"I have often wondered," said Joe, "why it is that a boat will sail better at night than at day."

"It is because the night air is damp and wets the sails," I said, "and they draw better."

"Do you think that is what it is?" asked Joe.

"Yes," I said. "When I used to race small sloops we always wet our mainsail and jib before the race to make them draw better."

He considered this for a while in silence. "Maybe that would be the answer," he said at length.

We talked of the sinking of a nobbie with six men aboard her, all drowned, during the war. The war, of course, was the First World War, for the Second World War left the Irish untouched since they were not officially in it.

"They say it was a German submarine that sunk her," said Joe. "They gave the men no chance. But I do not think the Germans would do such a thing. They are not that heartless."

"Who else would have done it?" I asked.

"There was some talk that the English did it to blame it on the Germans," was the reply. Old hatreds die hard. Ireland had not fought seven hundred years for freedom against the Germans but against the English.

"There were four men drowned in curraghs off the skerries," said Tom.

"There were," said Joe. "They had no right to be in the boats. They had come to a fair and drunk too much porter

100

and they set out for Aran. Only two of the bodies were found."

"They had no right to be in the boats drunk," said Tom.

"Twas the publican who should not have served them," said Joe. "He knew they must get back to Aran. There is a new man owns the public house now, and he will not serve more than two pints to anyone who has to go in a boat. He is a good man, may God save him. He will not serve even his friends, though they beg him."

Finally we got to the project of hiring the *glaucóg*.

"Are you willing to take me to Aran?" I asked.

"I am," said Joe, "but I will need another man with me."

"I expect to pay," I said, "so let me know your price."

He thought for a while. "Would you want to stay some days on the islands, or would you come back the same day?"

"I think we will come back the same day. I would just like the sail over and back."

"Five pounds," said Joe (about fifteen dollars).

"That is fair," I said, and so we made the bargain.

But we never got to Aran in the *glaucóg*. We needed either a westerly wind or an easterly, and the wind remained from the north. Instead we sailed out into the Atlantic in a roaring northerly wind which flung the ocean at our starboard bow. I was allowed to take the helm, and with us was the other man whom Joe said we must have for our crew.

He was a man in his eighties, and before we went aboard he stood pathetically by the boat, quite as anxious as a little boy who is afraid he will be left behind on a picnic. He was so old that the rims of his eyelids were reddened by the years and the skin on the back of his neck looked like creased leather. His hands were swollen out of shape by sixty years of labor and his shoulders were stooped like the side of a barrel.

"We won't need anyone with us," said Tom, and the old man's face was shadowed with disappointment. I think he knew that there must come a day (and it would come soon), when he would no longer be permitted to go to sea, where he had spent most of his life. He was afraid that this might be the day—the very hour and the very minute when he would be turned away from the sea.

Joe looked at him a minute, and then turned to Tom and said seriously, "We will take the old man. We will not go without him." The old man smiled and got into the *glaucóg* and busied himself with the mainsail, moving much more rapidly than was necessary to prove he was still hale and had many years of going to sea ahead of him.

It was calm as we left the little harbor. The bottom was pure sand, so the sea over it was a pale and lovely green. But when we got out of the protection of the headland, the wind roared in joy at the sight of us, flinging down on the *glaucóg* so that she leaned over in the water and fought her way into the wind and the sea, dogged and gallant, for she was meeting an old enemy.

I heard again the old familiar sounds of sailing—sounds hardly heard on pleasure craft, which do not venture out of harbors or calm water, and the devil take them. There was the sustained hiss of the ocean rollers, which, broken against the bow of the *glaucóg*, swept down under our lee. There was the dull trembling of the rudder in its pintless as it cut its way through the water. There was the thud of the seas on our sides and the evil, high-pitched whisper of the wind through the rigging. And below these sounds, the groaning of the mast as it worked, despite the rigging, in its seat.

We passed a small island, hauling to windward. "It is there that I was born," said Joe.

102

"And I, too," said the old man. He pointed to a roofless building not far from the shore. "That was my house," he said. "My father lived in it, too."

"Why did you leave?" I asked, and the answer was: the storm. There had come the one storm more terrible than all the other storms. It had destroyed everything—wells, flocks, fields, houses.

After the storm, the women had waited for the men to make up their minds. Whatever the men said, the women would do. The men had looked at the fields which had gone, the drowned animals, the breached walls and the roofless houses, and gone to whatever boats remained and left the island. The sea had won. But only for a while, because, the old man said, some families were moving back to the island.

"Do you like it better on the mainland?" I asked.

"The life is easier," said the old man. "But it is not as good as on the island. On the island things were better." He did not explain what he meant by better, and there was no need. What he meant was that on the island a man felt himself in the great bosom of the ocean. The wind that came to him was uncontaminated by passing over any land. It was ocean wind and came from infinities of space. On the island a man lived conscious of great things and of little things, and of his utter dependence upon God. He had pleasure in the tiny pebbles and shells of the beach and in the great rocks of the shore; in the puff of wind so small it hardly bent the grass, and in the howling of the ocean storm, in the little ripples of the harbor on a summer's day and the mountains of glistening black waves of the winter gale which flung upon the rocks and shook the whole earth. On an island, a man does not feel himself superior to everything upon earth but knows his right size, and this comforts him. When I am in the middle of a continent far away from the sea, I feel that

I am being strangled to death; that I am caught in a great coffin of land and am being smothered, and what dies first is the soul. But on an island I am one with the wind and the ocean and all their joys and am free. So I knew that it was not the depression that brought Joe back to Ireland, but that Chicago was too far from the sea, and he had started to die there and saved himself only by returning to Connemara.

After an hour's sailing we came to the Skerries—a rampart of rocks rising as high as twenty feet out of the ocean.

They are the most formidable rocks I have seen, sudden and remote and gray in color, with edges as sharp as ripped steel plates.

On some of them no man is ever known to have landed, for the seas swirl and leap at their base so it is impossible to bring a boat close to them. When I looked at these rocks I was filled with awe, as if I looked at death.

We fished for pollack off the rocks with hooks baited with imitation eels. Pollack are a fish that will bite only on a slow-moving bait, so we had to spill the wind in the mainsail to fish. We caught four or five.

The old man was the most eager of the fishermen, counting perhaps the number of times left when he could engage in this pleasure. The motion of the boat was erratic off the rocks, and Kevin became seasick. No one made fun of him, as is usual when people become seasick. The old man sought to comfort him by saying that he had been seasick many and many a time.

"It is the best thing for you," he said. "The best doctor in the world. You will have good health now for a year." Kevin lay in the bottom of the boat and the old man took off his coat and put it over him. The sky darkened to windward, and Joe suggested we should put back. The shoreline was out of sight and also the island on which he and the old

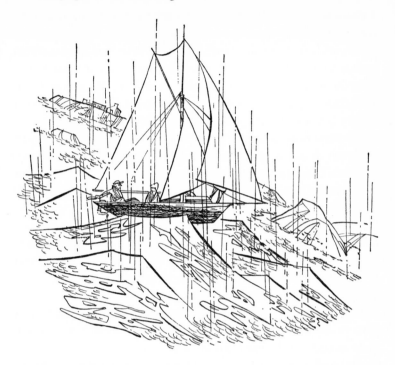

man had lived. A gloom came softly but swiftly over the water. Up to then the ocean had been a brilliant green. Now it turned the color of lead and the waves broke white like slashes of wrath. The noise of the wind, which had been but a whimper, rose to a piping note and the *glaucóg* fled across the darkened ocean for the invisible land which lay somewhere ahead in the scowl of the storm.

Joe turned to me. "Would you like more sail on her?" he asked. There was a glint of delight in his eye, and I caught the excitement—the wildness of the sea and the wind and the sounds of them about the boat.

"I would," I shouted.

We were carrying jib and mainsail and now set the foresail. The *glaucóg* heeled further over, flinging the spray over her shoulders. It came solidly into the boat but it was clean and good and exhilarating. The *glaucóg* was not decked except for a little piece of foredeck reaching back not quite to her mast. Joe was sitting on the thwart by the mast with his back to me, conferring with the old man.

He turned to me and pointed to port and, standing for a second, I saw a place in the black water half a mile away which was white tinged with green. Rocks. They had not been visible when we came out, but now with the falling tide they broke above the surface. I eased the *glaucóg* to windward and Joe pointed once again to starboard. I peered under the boom and there was another area in the black water which was white and angry. More rocks, then. And ahead there were some also—the fangs of the ocean.

Joe shouted their names. I do not recall them. They were strange and barbaric words, thousands of years old. But though every one had a name and its position was known, how would a fisherman know where these rocks were on a pitch black night with the wind hurling him towards shore?

"We know," said Joe, and that was all the explanation he could give. It is the kind of knowledge the hunter has when he knows that he himself is being hunted. It is a sense, and that is all that can be said about it.

On the way out, we had passed northward of the island on which Joe and the old man had been born, but now we skirted the south shore, the wind being too heavy to haul to the north. When we got under the lee of the island the wind abated, and we ran past a headland on which I could make out a ruined church. The old man took the halyard and as we passed the church he dipped the peak of the mainsail in salute. The church was that of a saint who had

106

lived on the island in the seventh century and fishermen passing have dipped their mainsails in reverence to the saint for
twelve hundred years.

During all our sail I had been left with the tiller. Usually
when you are sailing in another man's boat he will not let
you have the tiller without hovering over you and watching
the luff of the sail, giving you a hard look if you should
either come too close to the wind or fall off it more than
is necessary. But Joe had given me only one glance when
I took the tiller and then had gone forward, not saying a
word. He could tell in a moment I was a sailor and had no
need to worry, and I was greatly complimented at this.

But when it came to fetching the harbor, I wished he
would take over from me. The entrance to the harbor was
but fifteen feet. On one side was a concrete mole and on
the other a tower of rocks, and between them but fifteen
feet of water. Furthermore, the tide was falling fast and
I did not know what the bottom was like and the wind had
backed around so as to be dead ahead. Wind, falling tide,
an unknown bottom, and fifteen feet to maneuver. I could
just see the harbor entrance through the scud and shouted
to go about, for we were being carried down by the current
and could not make it. The *glaucóg* came obediently around.

"Let the old man take the tiller," said Joe, and the old
man came back, very serious and very pleased. We sailed
on the new tack for two hundred yards and then he put her
about again. We flew down on the concrete pier against
which the waves dashed and leaped upward. We were so
close that I braced myself for the shock, and told Kevin to
stay with the boat, for she might split but not sink. Then the
old man hauled the tiller to windward and we flung into
the fifteen-foot gap. He put his sea boot on the tiller, driving
it alee, flung out an anchor over the stern, and we came up

into the wind alongside the concrete pier in the quiet water of the harbor. It was all done in twenty seconds and the old man was grinning to himself and busy lowering the mainsail.

You are long for the sea yet, old man, I said to myself. You may be eighty years of age but the sea has not worn you out.

When we had made all secure, we went up to Joe's house for tea. We sat in the kitchen before a blazing fire of turf. The room was scrupulously clean. Even the bentwood chairs shone, and the light from the fire was reflected in the dishes on the dresser and the big delft mugs hanging in rows from shelves.

The room, painted in light green and yellow, was made gay by these colors. Joe's eldest daughter, who was ten, made the tea. He spoke to her in Gaelic and she cut the thick slices of soda bread and put perhaps two pounds of butter on the table. Then Kevin and I were made to sit down first at the table, being the guests. Joe and the old man went off to another room, and reappeared with their hair combed, faces washed and wearing beautiful knitted sweaters combining a variety of stitches.

"My daughter is only just learning to keep house," said Joe to me, to apologize for any errors she might make. Only the men sat at the table—the little girls had to wait for their tea by the fireside. That is the Irish custom. The men do the work, the men are out in the weather—the man's time is valuable. Therefore when they come into the house the women wait on them and do not eat themselves until their menfolk have been fed. The old man sat at the door where he kept looking out at the island where he had been born. He was deferred to in all matters. His cup was filled first (after my own and Kevin's as guests), and it was he who was turned to for judgment when any matter of disagreement arose.

"Do you know Martin?" he asked Tom.

"Martin Joyce is it?" Tom asked.

"Yes. Is he still alive?"

"Alive and hearty," said Tom.

"He must be an old man now," said the other. "I am glad to hear he is well. Does he still go out in his curragh?"

"He does," said Tom.

"He came over from Inishmor with me one time in a curragh. We landed on the Clare coast. It was a fine day. That was the first time I met him."

"How old were you then?" asked Tom.

"I was about twenty."

"How long is it since you have seen him?"

"I have not seen him since," said the old man. "But I am glad that he is well. Tell him that I am well, too."

"I will," said Tom.

"I would not like to live far from the sea," said the old man.

"It is a great delight," said Joe. "I can think of nothing pleasanter than to take the *glaucóg* out on the ocean on a good day and fish. It is more pleasant than to go to a wedding."

"It is the best thing in life," said the old man.

OFF TO THE RACES

11. FOR some time the talk in the evenings in
Finherty's Bar, where I would go with Tom or his brother
Pat or both after we had been out on the bay pulling a net
or setting a lobster pot, had turned to the Galway Plate.
Finherty's was a little bar directly in back of a grocery store,
also run by Finherty. In the grocery store one could buy
an assortment of canned provisions or cheese, or maybe
an egg or an English newspaper if you had such queer
outlandish tastes.

The bar was curtained off from the grocery store and its
floor was of rough old concrete. There was a short counter
on barrels, to provide the bar itself, and two benches against
the walls and a tiny fireplace. It was a dark kind of a place
but snug and unpretentious, and Finherty's stock was something amazing. He had brandies and whiskies, sherries, nips
of champagne, spiced Grecian wines, German hoch, French
Moselle and Italian chianti. I never saw anybody drink any
of these, but Finherty explained to me once that you could
never tell what kind of a strange thirst might overtake a
man, and so he had to be prepared for it.

But mostly he sold Guinness. This came so lively from the barrel, that it had to be poured first into an enamel jug, from which it was slowly decanted into a glass big enough to wash a bull in. Even so, at the first pouring, all you got was a buff creaming froth with perhaps an inch of black stout below that. When this had settled a little, the top was taken off with a wooden paddle and then more stout poured in, very carefully and gradually, until the froth was but an inch high on the glass, which was then given to the customer, the cost being, I believe, eightpence.

Most customers had a glass of Guinness from the barrel for their first drink. When the glass was half empty, they poured a bottle of stout into the draught stout, which gave a little life. It was considered a lack of drinking experience to drink a bottle of Guinness without mixing it with draught. For myself, I usually had lemonade or something of that nature, and Tom and Pat worried quietly about this, being sure it would shorten my days. They explained to me that people dying in hospitals were given a glass of Guinness a day and many of them recovered.

"It builds up your blood," said Tom. "I give a nip to the children once in a while." Guinness comes next to holy water as a preventer of evils in Ireland, but I never saw a man drunk in Finherty's.

"It is only young fellers who have no sense that take a drop too much," said Tom.

Anyway, for some time the talk had been about the Galway Plate, which is the greatest horse race in all the world, and I reflected that Kevin could hardly be expected to understand what made me an Irishman unless I took him to a horse race. This is the kind of pernicious reasoning which enables me to get through life without ulcers, for I am always prepared to bless anything I want to do by pretending that I am doing it for my children.

Tom said he would like to go to the Galway Plate, and so it was agreed. We would take Kevin and Tricia, and only such money as we could afford to spend, and in that manner nobody could possibly get hurt.

Off we went, then, setting out very early to reach the track a good two hours before the first race—when the best odds would be obtained for the main event, the Plate itself, according to the official program a race of two miles, five furlongs and "about twenty-seven yards." Here is the program description of the Galway Plate:

The Galway Plate. A piece of plate value 50 sovereigns with 1,500 sovereigns added, of which the second will receive two hundred and twenty-five sovereigns and the third one hundred and fifty sovereigns. A handicap steeplechase. A winner after publication of the weights (July 10th, 10 a.m.) of a steeplechase to carry four pounds extra; of a steeplechase value two hundred sovereigns seven pounds extra; of a steeplechase value three hundred and fifty sovereigns or steeplechases collectively value four hundred and fifty sovereigns ten pounds extra; of a steeplechase value five hundred sovereigns or steeplechases collectively value seven hundred sovereign twelve pound extra.

All this sorely puzzled Tom, and I had a hard time indeed explaining it to Kevin. The steeplechase part was easy—it meant a race with jumps, the name deriving from the excellent old sport of racing horses cross-country guided by the steeples of different towns. But I had a terrible job explaining to Kevin that if a horse won, he had to carry extra weight in the next race to make it fairer for the other horses.

113

"There's no sense winning, then," he said. "I wouldn't even try."

"If you were a horse you would," said Tricia. "Horses don't know any better."

The Willing Heart had been acting pretty well since we bought her, though possessed of some peculiarities. For instance, the windshield wipers would not work unless the front door was opened and slammed. Then they would work for a while, get tired of it and stop, when the door had to be opened and slammed again. It was raining the day of the races, and we progressed across the bogs slowly to Galway, opening and slamming the front door, which got Tom all mixed up trying to figure the handicaps of the different horses.

However, when we got to Oughterard, The Willing Heart decided enough was enough. The wipers stopped. I opened the door and slammed it, causing a rear tire to blow out with a loud report. This happened in the narrowest part of town, just past a bridge. I jolted the car over to the side and climbed out in the rain to jack up the rear wheel and put on the spare. But the jack wasn't large enough. Even standing on tippytoes, as it were, it wouldn't raise the axle high enough for me to put on the spare. I put a block of wood under the jack and the car promptly rolled off it. It would have crushed my head like a strawberry if my Guardian Angel had not told me to get out from underneath and tell Tricia pretty sharply this was no time to want to go to the bathroom.

Well, there we were with a wheel off The Willing Heart and the car resting on its brake drum in the road with the traffic backing up behind us, though in Ireland drivers have an astonishing good humor and patience and nobody blew his horn at me. Then a police sergeant came up. He was a grayhaired man, but he was a big man and would be stronger at seventy than I had been at thirty.

"God with you," I said, out of gratitude, really, to my Guardian Angel for Tricia having wanted to go to the bathroom and so saving me from death.

"God and Mary with you," he replied.

"The jack's too short," I said.

"You'll be in a hurry, no doubt."

"The first race is at two-thirty and it's one now," said Tom, "and we've hardly set our foot on the road." This was by no means accurate, for we had come a good twenty miles of our way.

"Who do you fancy in the Plate?" asked the sergeant, signaling a bus to make the attempt to get around us, which it did by pulling in its sides, I believe.

"Amber Point," said Tom.

"She's carrying nearly twelve stone," said the sergeant, "but she's a great leaper. I've heard a word dropped about Mazzibel."

"Have you, now?" said Tom, instantly deserting Amber Point and consulting the race card.

"What color is it?" asked Tricia, recovering from the rebuke.

"Claret with pink hoops," said the sergeant.

"Gee," said Tricia.

This was getting me nowhere, so I lowered the jack again and found another piece of wood and the sergeant turned to look at me with pity.

"Have you the spare ready?" he asked.

"I have," said I.

"Then I'll lift the car for you, and do you slip it on," he said as he got hold of The Willing Heart, lifted up the rear end and I put the wheel on.

115

"Thank you," I said.

"There's nothing in it," said the sergeant. "But I would think twice about Amber Point."

Off we went, and when we got to Galway it occurred to me I ought to get some gas. I drove into a modern gas station on the outskirts of town, and a harrassed man approached.

"Wonder if you could jack up that rear wheel and tighten the lug nuts, while she's getting gas?" I asked.

"There isn't a mechanic in the place," he said. "They're all off to the races and I've been left to serve the public." He spoke rather as one would expect a man marooned on a desert island to discuss his fate.

"Have you heard a whisper at all about the Plate?" asked Tom.

"I have not. Why should I concern myself with it when I'll see neither hoof nor hair of a horse this day through having to stand about here putting petrol into cars."

"The policeman said that a horse with pink hoops would win," said Tricia.

"I wouldn't doubt it," said the attendant. "Horse racing is the curse of the country. They'll be wives and widows weeping and wailing from Mayo to Kerry over the money that is lost this day."

"That's the truth," said Tom.

"People go out of their heads about it," said the attendant. "I had a fellow in here just a minute ago trying to borrow ten bob on his bicycle so he could have a whirl at the horses. It would make you sick to think of it."

"It would so," said Tom.

"And not a person left here to serve the public but myself and all on account of these same races."

"It will be lonely, all right," said Tom.

"It is a big responsibility," said the attendant. "For I believe this is the only service station open in the whole of Galway and if I were to close down there wouldn't be a drop of petrol to be had in the city—not even if the bishop himself were in need of it."

He replaced the hose, and when I had paid him, he looked around inside the car. "Have you room for one more?" he asked.

"I think so," I said.

"Then I'll come with you for wouldn't I be the biggest fool in the world to be standing here putting petrol into cars and everybody else at the races?" said the man. "Give me a minute and I'll close down."

He locked the cash box, disconnected the air hoses, locked the door and climbed into the back.

"The man with the bicycle that wanted to borrow ten bob on it said Fredith's Son would run away with it, even if he had to pull a garden roller," he said.

And so with the last gasoline station attendant in Galway added to our company, we arrived at the race track. The track lies perhaps two miles to the east of Galway, in lovely open, rolling country, and is reached from the road by a pleasant walk across a couple of meadows.

All of the West of Ireland and no small part of the east of Ireland streamed across the meadows—the women neatly dressed, the men in the rough-looking unpressed suits a size too big for them, common to the Irish. It seems to me that no man in Ireland, outside of the few city dwellers, ever buys a new suit of clothes. The country Irish seem to be always clothed in hand-me-downs, always too big for them. Children's clothes are bought with the economical notion they must grow into them. I recall as a boy how shop assistants pleaded with my mother to buy me a size larger

117

whenever a suit was being purchased so I would grow into it. How I hated these shop assistants, who condemned me to a life of hitching up my trousers and living with coat sleeves which came down to the knuckles of my hands!

Across the meadows, strategically placed in the path of the crowd, was a string of beggars of different sorts—a boy of nine seated on a stool playing the accordion; a man with withered limbs, plumped dumbly on the grass with a piece of waterproofing before him which was littered with pennies; further along a man with no legs singing of the glories of Brian Boru in a terribly cracked voice, and then an ensemble of fiddle, banjo and accordion flinging a jig into the teeth of the wind. Farther on still, there was a man in a raincoat collecting funds for the sixty-odd Irishmen who, a placard proclaimed, were held prisoners without trial or justice in the Six Counties.

And then the gypsies—the women with wild hair and thin faces and ragged babies, the latter gorging themselves on ice cream which besmeared their faces, or drinking what was surely sour milk out of soda or Guinness bottles. The menfolk, drowning in their tattered, oversize clothes, looked around with a sharp eye for some opportunity for profit, but the gypsies had nothing to sell and told no fortunes. Perhaps they had come because, as is well known in Ireland, the gypsies are great authorities on horseflesh, and might peddle a few tips on horses and so make a shilling or two.

The gasoline station attendant disappeared into the mob as soon as I had parked the car, and Tom proposed that we make a circle of the track and see its condition and what the jumps were like. Round we went, then, with several hundred others, discussing those jumps which had to be taken from an uphill approach and those which immediately preceded or followed a corner, thanking God that the track was dry and holding forth on which horses were good mudders and which were not. For myself, I knew nothing about any of the horses entered. But there was a hunger on the people for any kind of information at all about horses, and I found my own remarks were listened to with grave attention as though I had eaten breakfast that day with all the trainers. Tom was very anxious for tips, and whenever he saw a group of people, sidled up to them and stood close by straining to hear what they said. But I had long made up my mind how I would place my bets. I would leave the matter to Kevin and Tricia who, I concluded, probably knew as much about the horses as anyone else on the track.

The circuit of the track was something over a mile and a quarter of uphill and downhill going, with perhaps eight jumps, the finish being an uphill pull. There was nothing tailored about this circuit, no mowing and rolling of the grass nor softening of the jumps. There was more of the hunting field than of the race track; a good, hell-for-leather, jump-and-be-damned-to-you kind of a track that set your blood tingling just to look it over.

We did not go into the spectator area to watch the races, but squatted down inside the railings beside one of the jumps. I suppose we would have been hustled off by the attendants on any other track in the world, but in Galway it is different. The event belongs to the people, and they are not marshaled around and confined any distance from the horses and the jockies, but may sit upon the very turf along which the horses would soon gallop. There is an intimacy, then, between jockey, trainer and spectator at Galway which is one of the pleasures of the place, and when the horses were led out for the event, they made their way through mobs of people as at a country fair.

119

I gave the race program to Kevin and asked him to pick a horse. He looked it over, and fancied Ballyowen Lime, a chestnut mare of little experience, and somewhat small to my eye. I fancied a six-year-old gelding, but was dissuaded from betting by Tom, who had heard that the gelding would not have his heart in it that morning.

I gave Kevin half a crown and told him to bet to place, and he came back with his tote ticket, which he promptly lost. He was still looking for it in the neighborhood of one of the jumps when the bell rang and the race started. I hauled Kevin back to the side and we waited. A terrible babble came over the loudspeakers. It seemed that some wretched horse called Capacity Bridge was out in front with So Needed second, and Archer fighting it out with Coral Star for third place. Ballyowen Lime was lost somewhere in the mob at the rear. Capacity Bridge flunked a hurdle, Hyperion Lad came up out of the pack to second, Coral Star was third and Ballyowen Lime was still unmentioned.

"There's my ticket," said Kevin pointing to a bit of white on the hurdle before us.

"Leave it," I cried, grabbing his arm.

"I'll get it," said Tricia.

I grabbed her, too, and just in time, for round the bend flung the whole field, the turf thundering beneath their hooves, the jockeys cocked like triggers over the horses' necks, working away with their quirts as if slapping flies, while the crowd roared and laughed and screamed and cheered, and I believe some of them wept.

And suddenly we heard over the loudspeakers the magic name, Ballyowen Lime. She had come up from sixth to fifth to fourth and cleared a hurdle to take second, a position she was contesting with a little chestnut mare called Georgina. In a second they were upon us, thundering uphill toward the last hurdle. The ground shook. The turf flew. The field came to the hurdle and went over it like a pack of rabbits, waggling their hindquarters with glee as they cleared the barrier. I have never seen such joyous jumping in all my life. Not a horse faltered nor changed stride but over they went to the finish, flinging clods of dirt behind them.

They had hardly gone by before Kevin was out on the track and got his ticket. Ballyowen Lime placed third and I sent Kevin off to collect his winnings, which amounted to a shilling—a return of nearly fifty per cent on his original stake.

The second race was a flat race, and Kevin and Tricia picked horses which, as Tom explained, had been put in the field only to get in the way of their betters. They did nothing for us.

The third race was the main event of the day—the Galway Plate, with a field of eighteen—and Tom left us to circle nervously around the various groups of people, picking up a hint here and a hint there, and getting more and more confused. For myself I put the card before the children, gave them each a bottle of lemonade, and invited them to pick the winner. A few people, slightly appalled, gathered around to watch. Kevin looked the names over and didn't like the sound of any of them. Then he looked over the numbers and said he wished to bet on Number Thirteen to win. Number Thirteen was Highfield Lad, a seven-year-old gelding carrying a hundred and thirty-six pounds and without any experience in this steeplechase that I could trace.

"What about Mazzibell?" I said, recalling the earlier conversations that day.

"Won't do a thing," said Kevin, taking a good pull on his lemonade.

"If that's the horse with the pink hoops," said Tricia, "I want to bet on it."

"Win or place?" I asked.

"What's that mean?" asked Tricia.

"Holy Mother of God," said one of the punters, "how old is she?"

"Almost eight," I replied.

"Isn't it wonderful how some of them remain innocent so long," he said. I decided that Tricia ought to hedge and bet to place. For myself I picked Amber Point—the favorite—and Tom returned to report that he had heard some very encouraging things about Fredith's Son, and some more very encouraging things about The Major, and he didn't know what to do. Kevin told him to bet on Number Thirteen, and there was a consultation among the people around, after which they all went off to bet on Number Thirteen. The odds on Number Thirteen, Highfield Lad, now began to tumble a little, though whether Kevin had anything to do with this, I do not know. Stranger things have happened at the Galway race. From being an outsider at sixteen to one, the odds had tumbled to six to one by the time the starting bell rang.

We went up to the grandstand to watch this race. It was, as I have mentioned, a double circuit of the track, being of two miles, five furlongs and about twenty-seven yards.

When the field got away, none of our horses were anywhere in the lead. Two, but not ours, went down at the first jump and the others flung over them like hail. Another was eliminated at the water jump and another at a fence half a furlong further on, and then came the news that Amber Point was in the lead.

"Not for long," said Kevin. "Come on, Highfield Lad."

Highfield Lad, being then a quarter of a mile away, took no heed. He was somewhere in the first group but it was Amber Point, Knight's Brook and Monsieur Trois Etoiles as the race went into the second mile. And then suddenly it was Mazzibell—Mazzibell coming up from fourth, Mazzibell now third, Mazzibell, with a magnificent leap, taking second place at the water jump and then as they came into the home stretch, Mazzibell ahead of the field, pink hoops and all, and going like glory.

But then something happened to Mazzibell. He cleared the last jump magnificently and plunged onward with Highfield Lad on his tail, and then his pace slacked and some of the spirit went out of the horse so that Highfield Lad swept by to win by a full length, in the last twenty-seven yards.

And Mazzibell, coming in second, fled past the post, stumbled—and fell.

There was a shocked silence from the spectators, and then over the broadcast system a request for a vet on the track. The jockey examined Mazzibell and then, his face grim, undid the girth and pulled the saddle off. He put the saddle over his arm and walked silently to the stables.

"What happened?" demanded Kevin.

"I don't know," I said. "He's hurt."

"He's dead," said someone nearby. "Broke his back at the last jump."

"Impossible," I said. "How could he go that distance with a broken back?"

"Well, he's dead anyway."

"I'm going to find out," said Kevin, and off he went. I followed and found him talking to the owner.

"Is Mazzibell all right?" asked Kevin.

"No," said the owner.

"Is she dead?"

"Yes."

The owner looked at me and I nodded.

"Would you like to see him?" he asked.

"Yes," said Kevin.

He led him round to the back of the stables where Mazzibell was lying on the grass. We stood aside and Kevin went over and knelt down beside the horse. He looked very small and patted the shoulder once or twice and stroked the silky chestnut hair. Then he got up and looked at the owner. His face was white and I knew that if anybody said a word, he would break into tears and he didn't want to do that. The owner knew it, too, because he didn't say anything. They just looked at each other across the horse and then Kevin walked away. I knew that he wanted to be alone for a while, so I went off to find Tricia, whom I had left some distance off. She burst into tears.

"Darling," I said, "you mustn't cry. Everybody has to die someday, and it was much better for Mazzibell to die doing his very best to win a race. That is the way a champion dies—in the middle of conflict, determined to win."

"It isn't that," said Tricia through her tears. "It isn't that at all. All those poor people saved up their money and bet on that old horse and it went and died on them." And she burst into tears again.

There was no display of public sentiment over the death of the horse—no lowering of flags or even an announcement over the broadcast system. Mazzibell had come in second and died—the final twenty-seven yards had proved fatal, for her spleen was ruptured—and the bookies and the tote paid off and the next race was announced. In England or the United States, perhaps, there might have been some mark of sentiment, but in Ireland they went on with the racing. A horse is a horse—something different from a human —and no emotion is spent on the death of a horse even in dramatic circumstances.

Kevin having picked the winner of the Galway Plate, and an outsider at that, now became something of a mark among the punters. Wherever he sat down to examine the race card, there was soon the same little crowd of people around him—appalled by his methods but nonetheless impressed. Nor had he lost any of his touch. He picked money horses in the fourth and fifth event, and the winner of the sixth, and adding up the results at the end of the day he had tripled the small amount of money I gave him to bet with. Tricia had lost three shillings but enjoyed every moment of it, and I lost my shirt. Tom had come out about even.

On the way home I decided to give Kevin some advice.

"Listen," I said. "Never bet on anything at all if you need the money."

"Don't worry," he said. "I had five shillings of my own when we came here and I still have them."

"What were you saving them for?" I asked.

"Dinner," he replied. "Just in case you lost your head, Daddy."

THE RAGGLE–TAGGLE GYPSIES–O

12.   ALL over Ireland the tinkers wander and provide at one and the same time a mark for the charity and suspicion of the Irish people. They travel the roads in large or small bands, sometimes just a cart or two drawn by a horse or pony, and sometimes several caravans accompanied by a flock of horses and a flock of children. In the evenings they settle outside a village by the roadside, turn their horses loose to graze on the roadside grass and their children loose to beg milk or money from the villagers. The elder women help with this begging, carrying a plump, dirty but healthy baby to promote charity. The Irish, in all truth, are poor enough. And yet they can usually find something to give to the tinkers who, they will tell you, are great thieves, much addicted to drink and to fighting. There is no personal contact between the Irish and the tinkers. Christian doctrine demands that the tinkers be given alms. Self-respect demands that there be no other communication with them.

I had long wanted to meet these people but, abundant as they are, it is hard to meet them on any mutual terms. Common ground is not to be found between the tinker and

the non-tinker. Once, driving to Thurles from Galway, I saw two or three caravans parked in a field, stopped my car and went over to talk to the occupants. A woman with the face of a Madonna and flaming red hair stood at the open front of one of the caravans. Three little mites were playing under the bellies and around the hooves of the horses.

Seeing me approach, the tinker madonna reached down and jerked the children up into the safety of the caravan, holding them by fists no bigger than mushrooms, until she had them stowed safely behind her.

"Good day, ma'am," I said.

"Good day, sir," she replied.

"I am a writer," I said, "and I would like to know something of how you wandering people live."

"We are honest people, sir."

"I do not doubt it," I said. "But how do you make a living?"

"Mostly by begging," she replied. She immediately realized that here was an opportunity not to be missed, and picked up one of the tots and thrust him in her shawl.

127

"Couldn't you spare a copper, sir," she said, "to put strength in the little one? God will remember it and bless you if you give a penny now in His name."

I gave a shilling, but that was the end of our interview. The woman had firmly established the differences between us, and in doing so, had made a profit. I retired to seek my information elsewhere.

The next person I questioned about the tinkers was a priest, for the country priests of Ireland know a great deal of what goes on in the land.

I had many questions. The first of these was: do the tinkers marry according to any church or civil formula, or do they just take common-law wives? Again, where are their children born—in a hospital, a caravan or some ditch? Who attends the mother on childbirth? Are the children baptized, or brought up without religion? And, do the children get any schooling, or are they brought up illiterate, doomed to follow the roads, bringing up more children in ignorance?

The priest supplied some of the answers.

"They are not heathens," he said, "but Catholics, and they make excellent friends. When I was a boy I lived in Waterford, and often a gypsy family camped in a field on my father's farm. I became friendly with them. Then I went away to school and college, was ordained and appointed to a remote parish. One day my housekeeper came to me and said there was a gypsy at the door who wanted to see me. I went out, and it was one of my old friends from my boyhood days in Waterford. He knew all about me—where I had gone to school and when I had been ordained and that I had been appointed to this particular parish. Finding himself in my neighborhood, he walked twenty miles to see me. Others of my friends would hardly come ten miles, and they have automobiles."

128

"Do they steal?" I asked.

"Yes. A few hens or eggs if they need them. Maybe a bicycle. But they do not hold up banks or rob people on the road. They are not criminals."

"How about marriage? Do they marry in a church?"

"Yes. Sometimes, however, it is difficult and they have to wait a long time. A man came to me once saying he would like me to marry him to a particular girl from another tribe.

"I had to establish whether there was any consanguinity, and that was a difficult thing to do. I asked the young man where he was born and where the girl was born and who had been their parents. He gave me the answers, and then I asked him who could testify that he was not related to the girl. He mentioned the name of a tinker I knew pretty well. I told the young man to come back in a couple of months after I had made further inquiries.

"When he had gone, I sent word to the tinker he had given as a reference, asking about the young man and his betrothed. . . ."

"How did you send word?" I interrupted.

"By another tinker, of course. You can send messages all over Ireland through the tinkers if you know them, and they are always faithfully delivered. The answer I got back was satisfactory, and when I had checked with the priests in the parishes where the two were born, I was able to marry the couple. Before the wedding I cautioned them against too lavish a celebration, and they behaved very well—except the best man."

"What did he do?"

"The bride dropped her purse after the wedding. It fell open and revealed a considerable quantity of money. The best man immediately snatched it up and dashed out of the public house with it, so that the wedding party was marred by the need to pursue the best man and recapture the bride's dowry."

"When they die, where are they buried?"

"In a churchyard like other people."

"Would you trust a tinker around your household?"

"If he were a friend of mine, I would trust him with my life," said the priest.

The next person I asked was a police sergeant. My questioning took about the same form.

"Do they steal?" I asked.

"Arrah, they do every now and then. But nothing much—and haven't they a right to live like everybody else?"

"Do they go to hospital to have their babies?"

"They do not," he replied. "They have them in their caravans or under their caravans, for they do not trust doctors any more than you or I. I remember once there was a caravan with some tinkers in it at the other end of the town and they had been there some days, so I called on the man and told him that I would be obliged if he would move down the road a piece and not be staying so long in one place. 'Give me a day or two more,' he said, 'for my wife is to have a baby.' I could see that he spoke the truth, and so told him to stay and nobody would bother him. And she had the baby that very night under the caravan and an hour later was standing in the public house drinking a pint of porter and the baby nursing as pleased as could be."

"The people you see on the roads in caravans—are they gypsies or are they tinkers?" I asked.

"Sure, they're neither one nor the other. I don't think there are any gypsies left in Ireland. You'd have to go to Wales to find them. And Woolworth's has done away with the tinkers."

"Woolworth's?"

130

"The same. They were traveling tinsmiths in the old days and would mend a broken kettle or a leaking pot for you for sixpence. But you can buy a new one now so cheap that nobody bothers to get them mended any more. And that put an end to the tinkers. I doubt there's a man on the road in Ireland today who could mend a leaking kettle for you, though there was plenty of them when I was a boy."

"Well, how do these people that are called tinkers or gypsies make a living?"

"The men will get a day or two of work on a farm, and the women and children are sent down the road to beg. Then in the evening they all get together and see how much they have made."

"I thought they wouldn't work."

"They'll work when they have to," said the sergeant. "They've more sense than you and I. We work all the while to stay in one place, and stay in one place because we have to work all the while. But the tinker moves about and has no rent to pay and no taxes and can pick up a little milk or a few eggs or some potatoes without doing a hand's turn.

"I remember one day I met a man in this town who was wealthy, and a bachelor with no relatives. He had just bought himself a new Jaguar, and seeing him coming down the street, I congratulated him on his fine new car.

" 'Will you come and look at it?' says he.

" 'I will,' says I, and he takes me to the car and shows me how he can charge the battery himself at night, and all the knobs and dials that's on the dashboard as if it was an airplane. Well, while we're sitting there, along comes a tinker, and he's about to beg the man for a little money in the name of God when he spots me and, knowing I'm on the force, off he goes, for 'tis illegal to beg in Ireland, which means that 'tis indiscreet to beg in front of a policeman.

131

"Well, when the tinker had gone, shuffling in his rags down the road, the man turns to me and says, 'I'd give this car and my house that's fully furnished and air-conditioned and all I have, to be that tinker.'

" 'Why's that?' I asked.

" 'He has three things in the world that I haven't got and never will have,' says he. 'He has health, he has a family, and he has freedom.' "

The story was too prosaic. I was disappointed, for I had looked for a better ending.

"I don't think he meant it," I said.

"I'll never know," said the sergeant, "for the man was dead of a heart attack in a week and the tinker is still walking about the roads of Ireland and as healthy-looking a man as you're likely to see."

The sergeant told me that the only time the tinkers had been brought under any semblance of control had been during World War II when, in common with the rest of the people in Ireland, they had become eligible for ration cards for certain foods—mostly sugar and flour. At first the tinkers didn't care about ration cards, and there was the formidable problem of rounding them up and issuing the cards to these wanderers. And where should they collect their rations, when there was no certainty in what town they would be nor in what numbers?

The problem was partially solved by a gentleman in Thurles, the manager of a factory, who interested himself in the tinkers. He undertook to get all the food which had been allotted to them and issue it to those who called with their ration cards. Soon every tinker tribe made a point of calling at Thurles for their rations. Not that they needed them. Rather, they were able to peddle the amount of sugar and flour issued to them at black-market prices and so add to their income—as many more respectable people did. If you were short of a pound of sugar during the war, you could likely get it from a tinker, provided you were prepared to pay his price.

I had observed in traveling around Ireland that there is a great range in the status of the different bands of tinkers (or gypsies) I met upon the road. Some had nothing but a couple of miserable carts—the discarded pony carts and sidecars of a nation which has turned with enthusiasm to the automobile. Others had excellent horse-drawn caravans, painted for the most part a reddish brown, the spokes of the wheel pricked out in yellow and the sides of the caravans often tastefully decorated, sometimes with arabesques and sometimes with pictures of horse's heads, horseshoes, shamrocks and other such emblems.

I entered one or two of these caravans by invitation, and found them quite as neat as the interior of a New England cottage. All was clean as a bone, and copper kettles gleamed on their hooks against the wall. One caravan in particular had a beautiful polished water cask of oak. The cask was bound with brass hoops which gleamed like gold in the light of the lantern. There were little cupboards built into the sides of the wagon, the doors nicely painted in floral designs.

But even this family of tinkers (or gypsies) were not the elite. For one day I passed a tinker encampment consisting entirely of expensive motor trailers, drawn by very good cars. These people, I was told, were members of the great Shirtin family of Limerick, perhaps the most prominent of their tribe in the West of Ireland. Many tales are told of the Shirtins. It is said they are among the wealthiest people in Ireland, that they own several large houses in Limerick, have sent at least one of their sons to a college, and that one branch of the family, emigrating to America, became prominent among the bluebloods of Virginia or South Carolina (my informant could not say which). The descendants are well known for the excellent horses they raise on their extensive ranch in America.

To check all these stories, I sought a nun of the Ursuline convent in Thurles, Sister Dolores, who I was told has made it her life's work to care for the tinker children when they come through the town. She has a school for them, gives them both religious and lay instruction, keeps in touch with families of tinkers all over Ireland and is known to them all.

Plainly I must interview Sister Dolores, and so I drove from Galway to Thurles for this purpose.

But the facts about the tinkers of Ireland are not to be so readily laid bare. The first time I called at the convent, all the nuns had gone into a retreat during which they could talk to no one for eight days. I waited two weeks and drove to Thurles again. But once more I could not see Sister Dolores. She was engaged upon some work of piety and could not be disturbed. Circumstances were such that I had no time to wait until I could see her. And so I never talked with Sister Dolores about the tinkers, but had to turn once more to interviewing the tinkers themselves.

This, as I have remarked, is not a satisfactory method of getting the facts. But no other course offered.

I stopped my car beside a small family of tinkers on the road to Limerick, and immediately a slim boy in a suit two sizes too big for him left the encampment and came to me.

"Goll," he shouted to the others to warn them that I was a stranger. "Will your honor give me a cigarette in the name of the Holy Family, and I will remember you in my prayers?" he said.

"You do not have to pray for me to get a cigarette," I replied. "How old are you?"

"Eighteen."

"I suppose you are eighteen when it comes to smoking and younger than that when it comes to working," I said.

He laughed. "That's the truth of it," he said, taking the cigarette. "Will your honor spare a copper or two?"

Several others had now come up—two younger women, both with babies, two men, another boy and an older woman with iron-gray hair, and dressed in rags. She held the bloody hind leg of a freshly-skinned rabbit in her hand. All asked for cigarettes, and I obliged.

"Tell me something about yourselves," I said to the woman. "I am a writer and I want to know something about you."

"I will tell you the truth, your honor," she said. "By the Holy Virgin and all the saints."

"Well then," I asked, "do you ever tire of roaming the roads?"

"I am weary with it every day of my life, as the sweet Saviour is my witness," said the old woman. "But there is no other life for me."

"If you had a little house now," I said, "would you be content to settle in it?"

"I would, and I would never move a foot out of it but grow a few potatoes and pass the rest of my days in peace—may Christ Himself bear witness that I am speaking the truth."

"And if, the day after you moved into your house, the sun was shining and the air was warm?" I said.

"I would leave my little house for a while, your honor. I would indeed."

"And you would take to the road again?"

135

"Only for a little while, your honor. To catch a rabbit. Nothing else." She displayed the bloody haunch.

"How long have you been on the road?"

"Since I was born, your honor."

"And your parents?"

"Since they were born, I do believe, your honor."

"Did none of your family ever live in a house?"

"None, your honor."

One of the men now interrupted. "I heard that we had a house and land once, but it was taken away from us, your honor," he said. "In the bad days."

There was a clue to something here, for one of the rumors about the tinkers is that they are the descendants of people who were dispossessed during the many plantations of foreign stock in Ireland through the centuries. A method of paying the soldiers who invaded Ireland from the time of Elizabeth I on was to dispossess the native Irish and give their lands to the invaders.

"How long ago was that?" I asked, but the man did not know.

I asked about sickness and was assured that when any of the children were sick, a doctor was summoned. This I concluded was false, unless the sickness were desperate and beyond their own ministrations.

"You have some good-looking horses there," I said. "Where do you get them?"

"We buy them from farmers."

"I have heard that you take over horses which the farmers cannot tame and tame them," I continued. "Is that so?"

"Yes," said the old woman, "our men know how to handle horses."

"How do you train them when they are savage?"

"We train them, your honor."

136

(The rumor is that they muzzle a savage horse until he nearly drops dead from starvation. Then the man to whom he is to belong gives him a small quantity of food. Finally the horse learns to recognize that particular man as both his master and his savior. But the tinkers, though I pressed them, would not give any details of how they train horses.)

Finally they could restrain themselves no longer and asked me, in the name of the Lord, the Holy Family and all the saints in Heaven, to give them some alms. Those who had babies produced them, claiming that the babies were ailing, that there was no milk for them (two large pails of milk lay beside the wagons), and so on. I gave each of them something, and then some of those who had already received money from me, pressed me for more. At this the old woman turned on them.

"You have had enough," she cried angrily. "Leave him be."

That was all I could find out about the gypsies or the tinkers. I think it can be said of them only that they will tell you anything you wish to hear, and assure you by the litany of all the saints that they are speaking the truth. Though they have turned their backs on society, yet they are dependent on the tolerance of society and phrase their answers to ensure this tolerance. Thus, when I asked about the training of horses, they were aware there are societies which operate to prevent cruelty to animals, and so would tell nothing of their training methods lest they get into trouble.

They never take each other into court, but settle their disputes among themselves. They know every part of Ireland intimately—far better than any Irishman knows it. Every bit of road, every spring, every rock which will afford shelter from the weather is known to them. They know the disposition of the people in different towns and in different houses, who has died and who has moved, who is kindly and who is harsh. An encylopedia of information about Ireland, then, is available to them, but they will not share this knowledge with non-tinkers, and though you may, as I did, enter their caravans with permission, you will find out very little about their lives.

Thinking the matter over I came to the conclusion that the tinkers (or gypsies) are the remnants of the one-family tribes that once roamed the whole of Europe before the introduction of agriculture in the late stone age. They are all that is left of the prehistoric huntsmen, but now their quarry is not elk and deer and bear but fox and pheasant and domesticated hens.

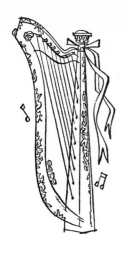

MUSIC
ON A MOUNTAIN TOP

13. THERE was a music festival at Lisdoonvarna, and Michael John suggested that it would be a grand way to spend the evening if we went there taking Tricia and Kevin, right after Sunday mass. (In Ireland the evening starts after midday and continues until the dawn of the morrow.) I agreed, for I have a keen interest in music and, having studied the violin for years, can play the "Londonderry Air" and the Ariosa of Bach, though in deference to Bach I never play the Ariosa in public. Furthermore, it is well known that the Irish are the world's greatest natural musicians—not even second to the Italians, Giraldus Cambrensis, in his survey of Ireland in the thirteenth century, having denounced the Irish under every other heading, had to admit they were the sweetest harpists in the world. And he was a Welshman, themselves good harpists.

So I was delighted at the prospect of going to the music festival at Lisdoonvarna, which was to be combined in the evening with several *Ceilis*. A *Ceili* is an Irish dance, and is the natural conclusion to everything in Ireland from cattle fairs to exhibitions of hooked rug work.

Lisdoonvarna is on the top of a mountain in County Clare. It is renowned for its waters, of which it offers a variety, all very good for one ailment or another. As we approached, we passed several truckloads of Guinness laboring up the mountain to the music lovers besieged at the top, and these, I was told, were but the tail end of a convoy of Guinness which had been taken there in the days immediately preceding the opening of the festival. Cars were parked for a mile on every road approaching the town and the streets were jammed with pedestrians. I do not think the turnout would have been greater if the Bolshoi Ballet were visiting the town.

We made our way on foot to the center of the town, for to drive was impossible. The mob was as thick as cattle at a fair, the crowd overflowing from the sidewalks into the streets—groups of young men and groups of young women, passing each other with titters of excitement on the part of the girls and simulated indifference on the part of the boys, this being the strange courtship rite common to rural Ireland. The crowd, as was to be expected, was thickest in the central square of the town. Here it was so dense that I concluded the artists must be performing on a platform somewhere in the square, and pressed through the mob to get to the center. But when I got there, it was to find only a man running some kind of gambling game. You bought a roll of paper with a number printed on it for sixpence, and a turning wheel selected the winners.

"You're exciting me," cried the man operating this game, his fist full of crumpled pound notes. "Don't excite me now. Is that you again? I thought you were supposed to be fiddling down in the barn?"

140

"Time enough for fiddling," said the man thus addressed. He had a battered violin case under his arm. "Give me one of them."

"You'll make more money and have more fun here," said the gamester, taking the sixpence. "But isn't the music grand, boys?"

The music was more than grand. It was overpowering. It was coming over loudspeakers strung around the square in clusters of four and along the adjoining streets. It consisted of a series of jigs and reels, played by a ragged but vigorous ensemble with a fine sense of rhythm, and to the devil with the intonation. Surely, I thought, there must be more offered than this—a town packed with people and Guinness, one wretched gambling game, and an intolerable torrent of reels as like each other as cowboy ballads, being squirted from the loudspeakers.

"Where's the music?" I asked the man with the violin.

He had other things on his mind for the moment. "I've won," he cried, showing his piece of blue paper to the gamester. "That will be four shillings."

"Where's the music?" I asked again.

"Over there," he replied with a jerk of his head.

I struggled through the crowd in the direction indicated, to find myself outside what looked like a large souvenir shop. It seemed unpromising as a musical salon. There was, however, a large and seemingly reverent crowd at the doorway and the sound of an excellent tenor voice coming through. Since none at the door seemed to wish to enter, I pushed through and found myself in a huge bar. The floor was wet with porter and waiters in shirtsleeves were carrying trays of the stuff here and there through a mass of men, every one of whom had a glass in his hand. Over in one corner, a man standing on a barrel was rendering "Hang Down Your Head,

141

Tom Dooley," assisted by an indifferent chorus. It was his voice I had heard outside.

"Stay a minute," said a man, seeing me turn to go. "There will be some desperate singing later." Since that was what I was afraid of, I made my way outside.

Michael John was grinning at me. Kevin and Tricia were sucking on the threepenny ices he had bought them, and since it was raining this seemed perfectly normal.

"Will we go down and drink some of the waters?" Michael John inquired. "They'd kill a parched horse but, sure, people come from all over the world to have a sup of them. 'Twould be a pity to miss them."

"All right," I said, and we set out for the pump room at the other end of the town.

We had gone but a part of the way when I caught the sound of bagpipes, and the crowd parted to make way for a pipe band marching grandly up the hill. I think they were playing "Bonnie Dundee" but it got badly mixed with "The Keel Row" coming over the loudspeakers. Furthermore, the pipers, not well accustomed to their work, which calls for lungs of brass, were handicapped in their efforts by having to march up a hill blowing all the while. The result was that all their top notes were flat, and I was astonished that twenty pipers should unfailingly hit E when F natural was certainly called for.

They were dressed in Scots kilts—the hunting tartan of the MacDonalds of the Isles, I fancy. They had somehow managed to get together twenty pairs of white spats, which might well have been surplus stores from the Boer War and had hardly been cleaned since, and they gave a grand parody of the slow gliding march of their Scottish cousins. The leader, out in front, swaggered ahead with a staff which I

142

fancy had seen many days' service driving cows and must have been astonished at its present occupation.

Behind the pipe band, clad in shiny blue serge suits and cloth caps, came the veterans of the Irish War of Independence. They had battered Lee-Enfield rifles and shotguns on their shoulders, and though the pipe band might have been a parody, the men who followed them looked authentic and people in the crowd saluted as they went past.

I had, by now, got hold of a program of the day's events and discovered that the musical festival, which I expected would be staged in some central part of the town, was in fact being held in various hotels, where different instrumentalists were competing one against the other. The program I obtained was printed in Gaelic and therefore incomprehensible to most of the people in the town. It announced that, at the moment, a junior competition of *feadog Stain* was being held at one hotel. I was determined to hear it and set off to the hotel in question.

Outside the entrance to the hotel, and on the sidewalk, was a piano with the notice "Have a Go" over it. A gentleman, undisturbed by the pipe band and the loudspeakers, was "having a go" on the piano, mixing the Blue Danube with "Bonnie Dundee" from the pipe band and "Garryowen" from the loudspeakers. The hotel was as crowded as the street and the square, and the music of the street and the piano outside boomed into the lobby. I found a room where the *feadog Stain* competition was being held, paid two shillings and got in.

By now I had discovered that in Ireland nobody pays for children, so Tricia and Kevin got in, with their ice creams, free. Perhaps two hundred people were gathered in this large room, smoking and talking, so I assumed either that

143

the competition was over or that I had arrived during an interval in the program.

I was wrong on both counts.

The musicians were performing, pressed almost against the wall by the audience. And I also made the discovery that *feadog Stain* is Irish for penny whistle. For that was what was in progress at the musical festival—a competition by children on the penny whistle.

I don't think that outside of Ireland there are many who can play the penny whistle. If it can be classed as a musical instrument at all, it must at the same time be admitted that it is as unreliable as a stilt-walker on ice. The slightest change of temperature will hopelessly alter its pitch, and the condensation of breath renders it unplayable after only a few moments.

In the teeth of these handicaps, a girl of perhaps ten, with a huge bow in her hair, piped away on the penny whistle, producing notes which, because of the hubbub, could not be caught ten feet from her.

Occasionally the master of ceremonies would ask the audience gently to be quiet in fairness to the contestants. The audience had no intention whatever of being unfair to the contestants, and the plea of the M.C. was generally taken as being uncalled-for. Each one had paid his two shillings to hear the penny whistle competition. But it was beyond all conscience that they should not be allowed at the same time to pass the time of day with a neighbor, inquire the price of cattle and about the health of the family. It was their own two shillings they had spent, and a man does not spend two shillings to stand in the silence of a tomb, listening to someone performing on a musical instrument. At least not an Irishman.

"Will ye be quiet now," said a women beside me whose own little girl was about to perform.

"Is it Mary that is going to play this minute?" asked her neighbor.

"It is," said the mother.

"And isn't she the darling child?" said the other. "Isn't that the dress she wore for her first communion?"

"The very same," said the mother. "I made it from a pattern that Brid sent me from America. But Lord save us, I had to lengthen the hem three inches. The dresses are terrible short in the States—above the knees, if you please and she ten years old."

"And how's Mickey doing with his schooling?"

"Terrible. He can't get the Irish at all. Sure he failed his exams, and himself went down to see about it with the schoolteacher. 'What's the trouble with the boy?' he asked. 'Why, he hasn't a word of Irish,' says the teacher. 'The divil with the Irish,' says himself. 'Wasn't he marked for export the day he was born?' "

And so the conversation went on while Mary, whose frock had been lowered below her knees in the interest of modesty, piped on her penny whistle and the mother who had called for silence talked all through the performance and didn't catch a note of it. The contest continued in this kind of hubbub and, finding that the *beidlins* (violins) were being played in a nearby barn, we went there.

There was perhaps a little more respect for the *beidlins*, though not much. Performing on the penny whistle is hardly a spectator sport, and therefore few sought to get a glimpse of the artists.

The violin, however, is not appreciated to its fullest unless one has a view of the performer. Since there were no seating arrangements at all in the barn where the violinists were performing, the more enterprising members of the audience had climbed on the window sills to get a view of the stage. Others had found chairs to stand on. There was a shortage of chairs. I found one for Kevin (who is studying the violin), and he had hardly mounted it before he was joined by three girls in full frocks, so he was lost in the folds of their skirts.

I would never have thought so many could stand upon the limited space afforded by the seat of a bentwood chair—nor that a bentwood chair could support such a load.

It didn't for long. The legs spread under the strain, and as the first performer plunged into his étude, the chair collapsed, tilting the occupants off. Everybody shouted "hush" but there is no way for four people to fall off a chair pianissimo. They did it forte and held up the show for a while.

The violinists had an advantage over the penny whistle artists because their instruments could carry over the discussion of cattle prices, porter, the weather, and the last time Jimmy McTurk was taken off to the sanitarium. Indeed a violin, well or poorly played, will carry above any other instrument, making it necessary to play one well or not at all.

None of the performers tuned their fiddles as they stepped to the front of the stage to give their exhibitions. Rather, they waved to friends in the audience and exchanged a few pleasantries with those nearest them. The first batch were children under fourteen, and they held the violins in positions of which even Paganini had never thought. Some held them straight before them, at right angles to the chest, rather as if they were about to take a cup of tea off the belly of the instrument. Others aimed the scroll at the floor and stooped over it in the manner of a man sighting a rifle at a rat.

Bows were held at the frog or somewhere in the middle, according to the fancy of the player. And yet, even with the fiddles out of tune, with impossible postures and bows held in any manner, the fiddlers produced some very lively jigs and reels indeed.

There was a minor and painful salute to classical music in the form of a sonatina by, I think, Clementi. This was endured by the crowd, which grew somewhat silent during the performance, as though extremely embarrassed that anyone should have composed a tune so dull, and over and above this, that anyone else should have undertaken to perform it in public.

The artist—a young boy whose tight collar gave an unnatural glow to his cheeks—struggled through the wretched thing, and when he had done, all were relieved. He then broke into "The Stack of Barley" with variations, and "The Divil and the Farmer", thereby redeeming his position as a fiddler and giving the audience an opportunity to stamp their feet in time to the rhythm. One or two of the younger bucks cut a figure or two of reel and jig in the corner.

I do not recall who won the under-fourteen competition on this particular day. It was immediately followed by a competition among more adult violinists, of which two offered according to the program.

The first, having saluted his friends about the hall with a wave of his bow, rather like a coachman about to take the Dover mail out on a foul night, reeled off his selection of jigs and was roundly applauded. The name of the next contestant was called, but called in vain. Runners were sent out and appeals made over the loudspeakers but without effect. He did not appear.

I could have given a hint of where the absent violinist was, but held my peace. I suspected he was the same man who was out in the square, his fiddle under his arm, while he bought ticket after ticket in the gambling game.

Of other competitions, there was the accordion, bagpipes, concertina, clarinet and voice. All of these artists competed not only against each other, but against their audiences and the strident blasts of jigs from the loudspeakers, and against the people who were "having a go" on the piano outside the hotel. There was not a harpist to be found, the penny whistle having taken over from the harp as the national instrument of Ireland.

The day's program concluded with *Ceilis* given in various hotels, and as I drove home from the most amazing musical festival I have ever attended, the truckloads of Guinness were still rumbling up to the top of the mountain.

THE ROCK OF CASHEL

14. THE Rock of Cashel is situated in the south center of Ireland in County Tipperary. It is at this place that the Kings of Munster were crowned in pre-Christian days. According to legend, they had a huge palace upon the rock of Cashel, which juts three hundred feet out of the Tipperary plain and commands a vast view of the countryside. The High King Angus was baptized by Saint Patrick on the Rock of Cashel—the date was A.D. 450.

I wanted to see the Rock of Cashel, but more as a remnant of pagan than of Christian Ireland. The people of Ireland were pagans for much longer than they have been Christians. But there is probably no nation on earth more anxious to forget this dreadful condition which preceded the advent of the Britisher, Patrick. In Italy, Portugal, France, England —almost any other European country—the discovery of prehistoric remains is almost a source of national pride. In Ireland it is almost a source of national shame. The Irish seemingly would like to believe that even before Patrick arrived, they were disposed to Christianity, and lived almost according to the teachings of Christ. This is nonsense, for there were few people as cruel, as bloody, as treacherous and at the same time as poetic as the ancient Celts.

However, I went to the Rock of Cashel hoping for a glimpse of Finn and Cuchullain and maybe Nuada of the Silver Hand or Niall of the Nine Hostages. I tacked onto a guide who had three Englishwomen in tow and was placed in an exceedingly difficult situation indeed. He was Catholic, and the Englishwomen he had every reason to assume were Protestants. His was the task of taking these visitors through the ruined Catholic abbey and the Catholic church on the Rock of Cashel and telling them something of their history. And the history of the abbey and church was a perfect litany of burnings, torturings and slayings of Irish Catholics by English Protestants.

On the other hand, he was in a key spot for encouraging the English tourist trade, which is more important to the Irish than the tourist trade from America. (It is one of the ironies of history that Ireland, having obtained its independence from England, relies on English trade and tourists to balance her budget.)

And then I came along looking for pagan remains. "Are there any pagan things to be seen?" I asked.

"For the love of God, take it easy," said the guide, with a glance at the Englishwomen standing a little way off. "Haven't I more problems on me hands at the moment than Ike himself?"

"I suppose," I said, "you were in the States."

"I voted the Democratic ticket fifteen years," he replied. "Come this way and I'll show you the chapel."

The chapel turned out to be the real jewel of the Rock of Cashel. It was built by Cormac Mac Art, and consecrated in A.D. 1134. It is only fifty feet long and twenty feet broad, and its tiny doors and windows are like something built for a child. The Englishwomen looked at it and pronounced it Norman.

"It was built in 1134 before the Normans came, ma'am," said the guide.

"But the Norman conquest was 1066," said one of the Englishwomen.

"That was when they conquered England," replied the guide triumphantly. "It took them another hundred years to set about conquering Ireland. They'd never have gotten into the country if it wasn't for a woman."

"Indeed?"

"It was the wife of Tiernan O'Ruiarc who went off with another man, and didn't Tiernan go and fetch the Normans to get his wife back, and didn't the Normans take the whole of Ireland as payment."

"I suppose that was before Patrick had Christianized the people," said Michael John innocently.

"There's some will be pagans, whether they're Christians or not," said the guide darkly. "Do you notice anything about that nave and chancel, ma'am?"

The Englishwoman looked at the nave. The chancel was not central with the nave but built to the side of it, giving a lopsided effect. The Englishwoman said plainly that it was lopsided.

"And will you look at that window, too, ma'am?"

We all looked. The window aperture of stone had an arched top. But the window was set in it in the same lopsided way.

"Wouldn't you say now that that had been carelessly built?" asked the guide.

"I suppose there was a reason for it," said the English-woman, cautiously.

"There was indeed, ma'am," said the guide. "It's a symbol

of the Crucifixion. The inside arch is off center because the head of Christ on the Cross leaned towards the left where his Mother was standing beside him. So the nave and chancel are a representation of the Crucifixion and so is the window."

Once the symbolism had been pointed out to me, the lopsided chancel and nave became immediately both touching and beautiful. The Cathedral of Cashel, which was founded in 1169, is side by side with the Chapel of Cormac Mac Art, yet the walls, within a few feet of each other, are not parallel, and the reason is as touching as the lopsided chancel and nave.

The Chapel was dedicated to Saint Patrick, whose feast day is observed on March 17. It was therefore built so as to be precisely in line with the points on the horizon at which the sun rose and set on that day. The Cathedral, however, was dedicated to the Virgin Mary. Her feast is May 1, and the Cathedral was built to be in line with the points at which the sun rose and set on May 1. The two buildings, therefore, diverge slightly from each other, bearing witness in their differing positions to the saints to which they are dedicated.

The cathedral for so venerable a building is by no means impressive. There are a few tombs about, but on most of them the inscriptions are completely worn off.

The top of one served as a public ash tray. There were innumerable cigarette butts, burnt matches, empty packets of cigarettes and candy-bar wrappers on it the day I visited the place, and the only name I could decipher was "J. ODwyer.", written in a loose scrawl by some holidaying vandal.

The floor of the abbey was not paved. Perhaps there is a paving lower down, but at present it is covered by an ugly gray limestone gravel, loose and dusty and not easy to walk on.

On the floor before what was the high altar are the graves of perhaps a score of archbishops and in the wall to one side is the tomb of Archbishop Myler McGrath, a scoundrel who had lived to be a hundred, had two wives and according to contemporary accounts "kept his church like a hogsty."

On this tomb is a curious Latin epitaph which the guide translated for us as follows:

> *The Ode of Myler, Archbishop of Cashel, to the way-*
> > *farer:*
> *In olden times there came first to Down*
> *The most holy Patrick, great glory of our land.*
> *To him succeeding, would I were as holy as he*
> *On the first occasion I was Bishop of Down.*
> *But for fifty years I followed thee, England,*
> *During the wars I pleased thy rulers,*
> *Here where I am laid I am not—I am not where I am not.*
> *I am neither in both places but I am in each place.*
> *The Lord is He who judgeth me—*
> *Let him who stands take heed lest he fall.*

While he translated this curious piece, the guide kept his eyes firmly upon the ground, for the epitaph contained some taint of anti-English sentiment.

"He was like the Vicar of Bray," he said. "He changed his religion to suit the times and was rewarded with the Archbishopric of Cashel by Queen Elizabeth."

"Perhaps he believed in the Protestant religion," suggested one of the women.

"Perhaps he did, ma'am," said the guide, anxious not to offend. "But wasn't it a grand thing that after fifty years of living off the fat of the land and marryin twice, he repented it all in the last minute and died in the arms of the true church?"

We were now before the high altar and the guide was faced with the most painful of his duties, for we had arrived at the Cromwellian period in the Cathedral's history.

"You'll have heard of Cromwell," he inquired cautiously, and the Englishwomen stiffened. One of the undoubted burdens the English have to bear, and will have to bear for all time to come, is the recital of the misdeeds of Oliver Cromwell in Ireland.

"Well," said the guide, "on the spot that you are standing and down through the main body of the church, Cromwell's soldiers massacred three thousand men, women and children, September 12, 1647."

Of course he didn't mean that. You could not get three thousand people into the abbey.

What he meant was that three thousand had been massacred in the town of Cashel at the foot of the Rock and several hundred had fled before the bloody pikes and swords of the soldiers, scrambling up the Rock in terror to seek sanctuary in the Cathedral. Most of those who fled the massacre in the town had been women and children, not men. The men had put up the kind of fight they could in the town. And when they had been slaughtered, the soldiers turned on the Cathedral, battered down the doors and started the butchery again while the women hid their terrified children behind their skirts and begged they should be spared.

But they were not spared.

"Nits will make lice," was the cry of the men of Cromwell, and the children were spitted on the pikes, too, in horrid death until the floor of the Cathedral was a carpet of mutilated corpses over which the soldiers had difficulty in moving to get the few survivors.

The blood streamed down the floor and out the doors of the Cathedral, down the steps and down the Rock to the town below. There was a river of it and much of it was splashed against the walls.

In the massacre twenty priests were slain. Three of them were killed before the altar, and one, Father Barry, was tortured to death. The soldiers demanded that he strip himself naked before his dying flock, and refused to do so. He was then bound to a pillar of the cathedral and burned for two hours over a slow fire until all the lower parts of him were consumed though he still lived. At the end of the two hours when there was still the movement of prayer on his lips, one of the soldiers, more merciful than his companions, dispatched him with a sword thrust.

And that was the great Cromwellian massacre at Cashel, one of a series of such massacres which has left the Irish hating Cromwell, and through Cromwell all thought of English rule, to this day.

This, however, was not the only occasion when the Cathedral was sacked. It was burned over a hundred and fifty years previously by the Irish Earl of Kildare, who was the deputy of Henry VII. He explained he had burned it in the belief that the Archbishop was inside, and the explanation was sufficient to clear him of the charges against him.

The final ruination of the Cathedral came around 1749 when the Protestant Archbishop decided to take off the lead roof. He said he would use the lead to rebuild a church in the town below, so that elderly parishioners wouldn't have to climb to the top of the Rock to attend divine service. But actually he pocketed most of the money. Roofless, the Cathedral soon fell into ruins, and it is now only a shell.

Yet it has a few interesting details. In one of the walls

flanking the high altar, I spotted a slit of a window cut at an angle facing the place where the tabernacle had stood.

"What is that?" I asked.

"The leper's squint," said the guide.

"Leper's squint?"

"Yes. The crusaders brought leprosy back with them from the Holy Land. The lepers had to attend mass but could not mix with the congregation. So they were put up there, and peered at the altar through the window."

I could readily picture the ravaged face of the leper peering out—a man imprisoned in stone and cut off for the rest of his life from his fellows, hungry for a glimpse of them. He would hardly have missed a single mass.

On a pedestal on another wall I spotted a small statue of a naked woman in an advanced stake of pregnancy. The face was gaunt and stared madly down at me.

"What's that?" I asked.

The guide blushed. He was plainly embarrassed, and led me away from the English ladies. "This is a very vulgar thing," he said.

"But what is it?" I persisted.

"Well, tis a fertility symbol from the old pagan times." He was now very red in the face indeed.

"Is anything known about it?"

"Well, it was found here on the rock when they were doing some digging. But it is really nothing at all. It is supposed to be a statue of a woman who was a very bad case indeed. She had no modesty at all and went around very shamefully dressed. That was in the time of the druids, before the coming of Patrick. Well, the druids were not bad men and they were scandalized at her goings on and they decided to make an example of her. And so they had that statue made of her, as you see it, and exhibited in public, so that the woman was shamed into decent behavior."

Having thus given to the druids a high moral sense which would undoubtedly have appalled them (they were great hands at burning naked virgins in wicker cages as a sacrifice to their gods), the guide dismissed the statue, which is probably the most ancient relic of the Rock of Cashel and may well be one of the most valuable pieces of prehistoric statuary in northern Europe.

"Are there any more prehistoric relics to be seen?" I asked.

"There's one," he said and led me outside to a large block of white stone roughly shaped into a cube. "That's the old coronation stone of the Irish kings."

On one side of the coronation stone a series of faint concentric circles can still be seen. I pretend to no knowledge of these things, but it struck me that these might represent the sun and have been the object of reverence of sun-worshipers, for both sun and wind were worshiped on the Rock of Cashel before the dawn of history.

Atop the stone was a large and beautiful limestone crucifix, set there, some said, by Saint Patrick. It was, of course, the symbol of the conquest of paganism by Christianity. It was also, it seemed to me, the symbol of an Irish determination to ignore or purify all that came before Christianity— which is a sure road to narrowness and ignorance.

At Loughrea, County Galway, there were some island dwellings of the first century B.C., and also a carved stone of the La Tène period, and I wished to see these things.

Loughrea is an anglicization of the Irish *Locha Riach*, which means gray lake, and it is a peculiarity of the little lake from which the adjoining town takes its name that, however bright the day, the lake has a grayish tinge to it.

The Irish are spendthrift about their antiquities. I would

hazard that there are more antiquities in one Irish field—particularly in the west—than there are to be found in many an English county or a French province. That being the case, the Irish know little or nothing about them. Sheep ruminate and cows graze inside the remains of thirteen-hundred-year-old monasteries. On the road to Loughrea I passed a field where the circular mounds of a prehistoric fort were plain to be seen, even by so inexperienced an observer as myself.

The fort, which may well be two thousand years old or even older, is a sheep pasture. It is probably well enough known to archaeologists. But archaeology in Ireland is a neglected science, and more is known about the life of the aborigines of Asia Minor than of the aborigines of County Galway. A great part of the unknown story, not merely of Ireland but of prehistoric Europe, may well be uncovered when a systematic excavation of Ireland's antiquities is undertaken. But at present cows chew their cuds over the graves of forgotten kings, and sheep scratch themselves on the disfigured idols whose names were too terrible to utter one thousand years before Christ.

I was not surprised when I got to Loughrea that nobody seemed to know that there were prehistoric remains of great importance in the neighborhood of the town. I asked first at the post office.

"Could you direct me to the ancient lake dwellings which I understand are near the town?" I asked the clerk.

He looked at me with gentleness. "There's nobody lives on the lake, sir," he said. "The trout season is about done."

"I don't mean now," I said. "I mean people who used to live there thousands of years ago."

"Never heard of them in the post office," he replied.

I suspected that I was not making contact, and emphasized that these were prehistoric lake dwellers, but the clerk shook

158

his head. Nobody in the post office had ever been called upon to deliver mail to the lake, and I retired feeling rather foolish over the whole incident.

I next tried at a bright-looking hotel—the sort that tourists would frequent. Surely the lake dwellings would be a tourist attraction and therefore the people at the hotel would know about them. But the people at the hotel, though sympathetic and anxious to help, had firmly turned their backs on the prehistoric. They could direct me to the ruined monastery or to the remaining portion of the wall which used to surround Loughrea, or to the new cathedral which is the most excellently furnished in Europe. But of prehistoric matters they knew nothing.

So I went to the *Guarda* or police. The Irish police are enormously helpful.

The constable on duty said he seemed to have heard something about an ancient grave which had been excavated just outside the town. This was going off at a tangent, but since the grave had belonged to the heathen times I thought it might have some connection with the lake dwellers.

He was not sure, however, of the location, and called the sergeant—a slight gray-haired man with the gentle eyes of a saint. The two of them conferred and agreed that if I went up a steep hill at the top of the town, I would find a gate and a cottage without a roof beyond it. Somewhere in the back was the grave. Also they gave me the name of a newspaperman in town who would know more about it, and directions how to get to his house, and pleaded with me if I was not successful to return and they would try again.

A house without a roof on it may be an excellent landmark in other countries but in Ireland it is one of the worst.

Ireland is full of houses with no roofs on them—sad little

two-roomed abandoned houses with roofs fallen in or blown off, standing there naked and desolate and full of nettles.

In this instance, I found three roofless houses on the hill in question. The most promising was reached by going up a boreen and, sure enough, in a field behind it and at the far end of the field, was a shed of the sort that archaeologists put over their excavations.

It was a long field, and when I got closer to the shed I saw it was made of discarded pieces of sheet metal, one of which had once been a sign advertising Gold Flake Cigarettes.

I found the entrance and peered in expecting to see a moldering hole with an exciting skull at the bottom of it, brown with age, and perhaps a stone war hammer.

What I found was the biggest black bull I ever hope to meet. I stared at him petrified and made a few whimpering noises like a rabbit before a snake, for I am very frightened of bulls. He stared back at me with contempt, and snorted. I fled, leaping over a wall into a cemetery (modern), grateful for a barrier of five feet of limestone between the bull and me. The bull did not even deign to come out of the shed in which I had found him.

The next roofless house stood in a field which I first surveyed to make sure it contained no animals. There were none, so I entered and marched to the roofless house which lay at the top of a slope. When I got near it, I heard a wheezing behind me and the tread of heavy feet. My bones liquefied and I turned around. But it was only a sheep. I am not afraid of sheep, so I gave it a piece of my mind for frightening me and looked around for the prehistoric grave.

But I could find none.

Some little distance off, I saw a house in a hollow and, thinking to get information there, I went to it. There were tattered lace curtains hanging in the windows but there was a great mournfulness about the place. I knocked on the door and the blows of the knocker boomed through the building. No one answered. The house was deserted. All that remained of the occupants were the lace curtains hanging in the windows, and I wondered in what kind of hurry or panic they had been to leave the curtains still up.

The house had a certain charm to it despite its melancholy. There was a little wood nearby and a stream flowing through it, and a place that had been a garden and another that had been a lawn. Lying in the hollow, it was well protected from the wind, and many children must have played in the garden or gone looking for bird's nests or rabbits in the little wood. But now there was no one there at all and standing outside the door was a perfect stranger, who had come six thousand miles to knock on the door of this deserted house to inquire about a prehistoric grave.

Then I passed a giant's house. There is no other way to describe it accurately. It was a house of only two stories, but the biggest house I have ever seen. From ground to roof it appeared about fifty feet high, so that the windows were enormous and the rooms must have had twenty-five foot ceilings. It also was deserted. I could see through the gigantic windows into the gigantic rooms, and noted that the giants who used to live there had been partial to wall-paper with a gigantic flowered pattern. Crows, no bigger than flies, circled around the roof. The structure towered over the landscape and as I went by I said to myself:

> "*Fee fie foe fum,*
> *I smell the blood of a Cornishman.*
> *Be he alive or be he dead*
> *I'll grind his bones to make my bread.*"

161

I felt fairly safe, being Irish, though Cornishmen are Celts too, and had their own language, which died out I believe about half a century ago.

Defeated in my efforts to find the prehistoric grave, I turned to Mr. O'Donovan, the town newspaperman. The country newspaperman is a neglected figure in the world of learning. Neither scientist nor scholar, and holding himself somewhat superior to both, he is the latter-day annalist of many a community, and combines with this role that of story-teller and local historian, though the history he unearths is recorded in his newspaper.

Mr. O'Donovan filled his role to perfection. He took me to his study through a little swarm of children, one of whose father, he explained, spent his time "fiddling with other people's money at the bank." In the study he opened a drawer of his desk overstuffed with newspapers, brochures, broadsides, photographs, handbills, memos and other material too valuable to be discarded, too extensive for use. Out of this drawer he pulled a newspaper whose front page was devoted to a speech by Parnell on land reform, a photograph of himself with a ten-pound trout, another of a prize bull, a broadside advertising an auction twenty years ago, the deed to a house (or such I took it to be), and finally a brochure describing a carved La Tène stone which was to be found near the town.

"What about the island dwellings?" I asked.

"You can't miss them, passing the lake," he said.

"You mean those little islands in the lake?"

"The same."

"Anything on them?"

"Nothing."

"And the prehistoric graves?"

"Never heard of any. There are some old stones on the

162

hill as you approach the town. During the Williamite wars the Irish put uniforms on them and held off the English for a few hours while they re-formed their army."

I said I'd go out and look at the La Tène stone. And so I did. It was in a sheep meadow, and richly carved. It stood only about three feet high, was dome-shaped, and the entire surface covered with a geometric design at once intricate and serene. There were four small plinths making a square around it, to protect the carvings from the sheep and cows in the meadow. And there was an exasperating plaque in Irish reminding people not to deface the stone.

But nothing else.

Of the people who carved the stone and why they carved it and where they came from and what happened to them, not a word. However, this was in Ireland and the Irish are indifferent to such things.

A WOMAN IN THE HOUSE

15. WHILE we were staying at Killron in Connemara, the greater part of our housekeeping was done by
Tom's wife, and that through the kindness of her heart, for
there was no understanding at all that she should do this.
After we had been there a little while, it gradually dawned
on me that some clothes ought to be washed, and so I told
Tricia to get together all the soiled clothes she could find,
as I proposed to do the laundry.

"And do not confuse me by saying you are not able to
find one-half of a pair of socks," I said, while Tricia stood
gravely before me. "Socks are socks, and in this part of the
world I doubt any scandal is raised by a man or a child
wearing mismatched socks on their feet.

"There aren't any soiled clothes except those we've got
on," said Tricia with a touch of superiority.

"Girl," I said, "do you mean to tell me that you and your
brother have been living this past week in the same clothes?"

"No," said Tricia, sweetly, "I knew you'd forget about
the laundry, Daddy, so I took the clothes over to Tom's wife

and she did the washing for us. They're all in the airing cupboard."

"What airing cupboard?" I demanded.

"Every house in Ireland has an airing cupboard," said Tricia. She opened the doors of a small cupboard in the kitchen the presence of which had previously escaped me. There, stretched on a line, was our clean washing. The air in the cupboard was beautifully warm, for the wall of the cupboard formed the rear of the fireplace in Tom's house.

This was the first time I fully realized that a seven-year-old girl has already developed instincts for housekeeping, and just as a son tries to some extent to model himself on his father, so a daughter attempts to enter the world of domestic duties of the mother. I must say that I was surprised, for I hadn't thought that Tricia was capable of much more than dressing herself, washing her face and combing her hair, though she can also lay and clear away a table.

I went to see Tom's wife, Ann, to apologize that my laundry chores had devolved on her, which I had by no means intended. She was busy in the kitchen baking a loaf of soda bread over the turf fire, and looked at me, her face full of silent laughter.

"The men aren't much different in America, now, are they?" she asked.

"In what way?" I asked.

"Sure a man lives in a house and has no idea what is going on about him. Tricia helped with the laundry and she's a great little hand with soda bread, too."

From this time on I began to see Tricia in a different light. Or rather I began to see another aspect of my daughter. She was capable, I knew, of flirting outrageously with me, and she had a frightening ability to coax a new hat or a new pair of shoes out of me. I recall that once she asked me to take her to tea in Galway, and I rather looked forward to the excursion, for she takes tea prettily, sitting upright in her chair, not squirming, and ordering the cakes with an enchanting mixture of delicacy and excitement. There was one restaurant in Galway to which we always went, and were quite familiar with the route to it from the parking lot. On this occasion Tricia, however, led me down another road, and we passed a large store which I was dimly aware sold frocks and such things.

I plunged by, only to be caught by the hand and brought to a standstill before the window.

"That's a nice red frock isn't it, Daddy?" said Tricia.

I agreed that it was a nice red frock.

"I think it's just my size," she said, and sighed patiently. I was vaguely aware that some kind of a crisis had presented itself but was not quite sure of its nature because I have little interest in frocks, and I was wondering whether after tea I could get around to the library and look up some material on an old abbey in the neighborhood.

"Yes," I said, "it looks as though it would fit you." I was about to go on when I noticed that Tricia was biting her lip, which is the preface to tears. And then I realized what a stupid, dull brute I was being.

"Would you like that frock, Tricia?" I asked.

"You're the best Daddy in the world," she said and jerked me through the door lest I repent. The frock was brought and it fitted Tricia to perfection.

"We won't bother about buying a new pair of shoes to go with it," she said. "I'll make out with these sandals."

So we bought a pair of shoes, too. We also bought a knitted bonnet with a bright bobble on it, and another frock for Arabella who is three and had stayed with Hazel in California. Then Tricia said I ought to buy something for myself, and I agreed that perhaps I could do with a new pipe. But she took me over to the men's department and I wound up with an Aran *crois*, which is a handwoven belt, wound twice around the waist and used for keeping the trousers up.

Then we had tea together, and the waitress (bless her heart) said the frock suited Tricia to perfection. Tricia smiled and blushed, conscious, I am sure, of a deep sense of achievement, for she had managed to get a new frock, a pair of shoes and a hat for herself out of a rather absent-minded father who paid little attention to girls' clothing. Reflecting on that incident later, it occurred to me that she must have spotted that particular frock on several occasions and had spent some time devising the tactic by which I would be persuaded by buy it for her.

A father catches only occasional and enchanting glimpses of the world of his daughters. With his son's world he is more familiar, having been himself a boy. But his daughter goes along a surprisingly different road and it comes as a shock to him at times that there is in every little girl a great amount of womanhood.

When it was time for us to leave Killron and go to Kinvara, I was concerned about packing. During my bachelor days, packing was the easiest thing in the world for me to do. I took only what was necessary and left the rest. Thus, when in my youth I left London for Port of Spain, Trinidad, British West Indies, I took several shirts and socks, a change of shoes, two suits and a Spanish guitar, leaving behind my furniture, pictures and other things which would only be an impediment. However, warned by Hazel that I had to apply myself seriously to packing and that everything was important, I saw a loathsome task ahead of me. Fortunately there was a report of mackerel coming into the bay at the time I should have started packing, so I loaded the children into the boat and we went out after them. Kevin took one pair of oars, I the other, and Tricia, who up to this time had not caught a fish, was allowed to take the line. It wasn't long before she had caught a beautiful mackerel, her first fish, but she was so excited I was afraid she would fall overboard, so I had Kevin pull it in for her. The mackerel run lasted a couple of hours and we caught a score or more, Tricia carefully putting aside the one she had caught herself. When we came ashore, we distributed the fish among those who wished them, keeping Tricia's, of course, and returned home. It was now much too late for packing and anyway if there is one law which is scrupulously observed in Ireland, it is that nothing has to be done merely because it is time to do it. So we went off to bed, I having comforted myself with the resolve to get up early the following morning and do the packing.

But when I got up, it was nine o'clock. I hastened downstairs to find that Kevin and Tricia had already eaten their breakfasts and were sitting on the sea wall watching the little crabs scavenging among the rocks in the water below. I ate a very unsatisfactory breakfast and hustled up to the children's rooms to start the packing. I pulled open one of the drawers of Tricia's dresser. Empty. I pulled open another. Empty.

"Tricia," I called out the window, "where in thunder are all your clothes?"

"They're packed, Daddy," she said with great composure.

And so they were, Kevin's also, and mine as well. Tricia had got up and done the packing, and done it magnificently, forgetting only a few essentials like my pipes and a couple of curious rocks I had found, and a piece of black Connemara turf I wanted to take back to California out of pure sentiment.

168

I didn't check the bags. I checked the house and found little that had been overlooked. When we got to Kinvara I opened up my bag in which Tricia said she had put the towels and other things immediately needed. And there, on top, was Tricia's mackerel, wrapped in waxed paper.

"I thought we would need it for dinner," she said almost tearfully. There was a pound of butter close to the mackerel, and an attempt at a union had been made between these oddly assorted foods.

"We certainly do need the mackerel for dinner," I said. "You were a good girl to remember it."

"I didn't know what to do with the butter," said Tricia, recovering her composure. "Mummie didn't tell me how to pack it."

"Butter is difficult," I agreed.

We had a wide choice of bedrooms in the house in Kinvara, which was much bigger than the one we had occupied in Killron. Tricia was allowed to pick her bedroom first, and after she took the prettiest, asked me to bring her bag upstairs. She promptly closed the door, and when she emerged later her hair was nicely combed and she had changed into the red poplin frock I had bought her in Galway. Kevin and I looked at each other. We were wearing jeans and flannel shirts and the jeans were none too clean.

"I guess we'd better tidy up for dinner," I said.

"Guess so," said Kevin, moodily. "What do you suppose has happened to Tricia?"

"Son," I said, "we are going to have to get used to the thought that there is a woman in the house."

THE CASTLE OF THE DISHES

16.   JUST outside Kinvara, there are the remains
of a castle which is known as the Castle of the Dishes.

"Why such a name?" I asked of Brig, the daughter of
Mrs. Gleason, the schoolteacher whose house we rented.

"It is because of a very holy thing which happened there
centuries ago."

"And what was that?" I persisted.

"Well, the castle belonged to King Guaire, and he was
a very hospitable man. He had a brother who was a very
saintly man, and this brother spent the forty days of Lent
fasting on a mountain top not far from here. He had with
him, keeping a fast, a small boy. The man was Saint Colman.

"When the end of the Lent period came, the King in his
castle sat down to a splendid feast of all kinds of food
served on beautiful golden dishes. But Saint Colman had
nothing to eat on top of the mountain and the boy who was
with him complained that he was very hungry. Saint Colman
therefore prayed to God that He should send something for
the boy to eat. Immediately, the dishes with the food which
had been set on the table before King Guaire rose in the

air and flew off up the mountain and were laid before the saint.

"Guaire was angry, and ordered his soldiers to follow and see where the dishes went. They mounted their horses and set off, but as they approached the saint, the stone mountain became soft for a moment. The horses' hooves sank in the flanks of the mountain, which immediately hardened. And if you go up the mountain you can see the hoofprints of the horses in the stone to this day."

When I heard this story I naturally did not believe it, though I was too polite to say so. But Kevin believed it and so did Tricia. For myself, I looked at the castle and seeing that it was of Norman design concluded that some grave error had been committed, for Guaire reigned in those parts some six hundred years before the coming of the Normans to Ireland. In short, Guaire and Saint Colman were dead six centuries before the castle was built. On the other hand, there was the remnant of a much older arch nearby, plainly part of a much larger building, though how old, I could not say.

The story, however, aroused my curiosity, and leaving Kevin in a field helping to tie sheaves of corn, and Tricia in a butcher store with Michael John's sister Oona, who was taking care of the shop, I went into Galway to the library to find what I could about the Castle of the Dishes.

I found a great deal.

The name of the castle is Dungory, which is an anglicization of Dun Guaire, meaning the fort of Guaire. Guaire, King of Connaught, had reigned from 604 to 642. He seems to have been overthrown, and one source said he died in 663 and is buried in Clonmacnois, but that is perhaps beside the point. He was a historical figure and his fort was outside Kinvara.

However, it was not the present castle, though undoubtedly it was built on the same site. There seem to have been three castles—one built by Guaire, which was demolished and another castle raised, perhaps using the same stones. This was captured by the O'Shaughnessies, who pulled it down and put up a third castle, possibly the one that remains today.

So much for the castle. The one revered as the place from which the dishes flew at the command of God was not even built at the time, as I had suspected. But there was still that puzzling old arch nearby which just might date from the seventh century.

I next looked up Guaire himself. In Kinvara the people knew that this man who had lived thirteen hundred years ago had been very generous. They could give no examples of his generosity except to say that had been his distinguishing trait. When I looked into the records, this aspect of Guaire's character was confirmed, for he must have been one of the most generous men to have lived in Ireland. According to the legends, his right hand was bigger than his left, for with his left hand he gave to the wealthy but with his right he gave to the poor. Once, viewing a large church with Saint Cummian and Saint Caimin, the men had put to each other the question: what would they like to have so large an area filled with?

"Disease," said Saint Caimin.

"Why?" he was asked.

"So that I might suffer all the sicknesses in the world in penitence for my sins," was the reply.

"I would have the church filled with books so that I might have enough to spread learning through the world, giving one to each person who desired knowledge," said Saint Cummian.

172

"I would have the church filled with gold and silver," said King Guaire, "so that I might have the joy of giving it away to all those who are in need."

The only time that King Guaire's hospitality was strained was when he entertained O'Curry, the Chief Bard of Ireland. When O'Curry came to visit Guaire he brought one hundred and fifty lesser bards and one hundred and fifty students, as many women, and several hundred servants and vast flocks of horses and dogs. Guaire received them all with open arms and installed them in his castle. The visit lasted for a week, then a month, three months, six months, and then a year until finally they had been there a year and five months. Still the multitude of guests remained, and gave no sign of any intention to depart.

The generous Guaire, though brought to the verge of ruin, was still too hospitable to hint to his guests it was time to move. He forebade anyone to treat even the servants of the Chief Bard harshly, though his own men were now on short rations so the innumerable guests should be provided with all they could desire.

Finally Mearbhair, brother of the King, hit upon a stratagem which would shame the Chief Bard into moving. The bards of Ireland in those times were the keepers of all the old legends and tales which they recited to their royal patrons and taught to their pupils. These legends were divided into about three hundred and fifty main tales, and one hundred lesser tales. They were also classified according to their subject matter: *Aite* (tales of death), *Catha* (tales of battles), *Echtrai* (tales of adventurous journeys), *Fessa* (tales of feasts), *Tana* (tales of cattle raids), and so on. Every bard had to know word for word each of these stories, so an apprenticeship starting in early childhood was required to become a bard or a poet.

173

But in Guaire's time there was one tale missing—the *Tain Bo Cuilgne*—the Tale of the Cattle Raid of Cooley. This had been lost and the Chief Bard did not know it.

One evening, therefore, Guaire's brother, Mearbhair, after a sumptuous feast, suggested to the Chief Bard, O'Curry, that he might tell a tale to the assembled guests.

"What tale do you wish to hear?" asked the Chief Bard.

"The Tale of the Cattle Raid of Cooley," replied Mearbhair.

"You shame me," said O'Curry, "for it is known that this tale is lost. None know anything but fragments of it and even I, the Chief Bard of Ireland, cannot recite it to you."

The following day, having been publicly shamed into admitting that he was not master of all the tales in Ireland, he left Guaire's castle.

But that was not the end of it, for the Chief Bard's son, determined to remove the shame from his father, journeyed the whole of Ireland seeking someone who could tell him the story of the cattle raid of Cooley. At last he came to the shore of Loch Ein in modern County Roscommon, and being exhausted, lay down to rest. He then recalled that Loch Ein was the place where the warrior, Fergus, a principal character in the tale, had been killed, and he begged Fergus to return from the grave and restore to the people of Ireland the full details of the Tale of the Cattle Raid of Cooley.

Suddenly he was enveloped by a shimmering mist, saw the ground open before him and heard the voice of Fergus telling him that a penalty must be paid for disturbing the rest of the Heroes, but if the poet were willing to pay it, he might hear the tale. The young man having said he would pay any price, he heard the rumbling of the wheels of the great war chariots of Connaught, the battle cries of the

174

warriors, the thundering hooves of the Gray of Macha which pulled the chariot of Cuchullain, the whistle of the spears through the air, the death cries of the champions and saw the rivers turn red with blood, saw the fairy mists which enveloped the battlefield when Cuchullain was in danger. Thus the whole tale was enacted before his eyes so he never could forget a single detail of it.

Then the mist which had surrounded him was dispersed, and he returned to his father and told him he had found the lost story. The bards of Ireland were assembled and the boy recited all he had seen. All those present could themselves feel the shock of battle, and wept when they heard that Cuchullain had killed the friend of his boyhood, Ferdiad, sent against him as the champion of Connaught.

When the last words of the tale had been spoken, the Chief Bard turned to his son and said, "You have returned to us the greatest of our treasures. What is the penalty which you are required to pay, for no penalty could be too much?"

But where his son had stood, there was only a pile of ashes so small it could be put in the shell of a hazel nut.

Here was a lovely legend linking the village of Kinvara with one of the greatest tales of Irish mythology. Nobody to whom I had spoken in the village had known of this link. But I found nothing about the story of the dishes.

Then the librarian produced a pamphlet published some forty years before giving the story, and it was basically the same as that told by Brig. The only difference was that when Guaire the Hospitable had sat down to his banquet on Easter morning, he had said, "Lord, grant that this food should be received by whatever servant of yours stands most in need of it." And the dishes had immediately left the table and gone up the mountain to Saint Colman and the boy, the King sending his horsemen to find out to whom the banquet was going.

I had established then that there was such a figure as Guaire, that he was enormously hospitable, that his castle had been close to Kinvara, and nothing else which could not be classed as legend. I left Galway, returned to Kinvara and visited the castle, ignoring the newer Norman structure and concentrating on the old stone arch.

The tide was out, leaving deep channels around the little tidal island upon which the ruins stand. Across these channels were one or two walls which Michael John told me had been constructed to trap salmon. The salmon came in on the flood tide and were caught behind the walls as the tide receded. There was a very deep place called the *Poll Mor* (Big Hole), in which the water was brackish. The water came from an underground spring and was rendered brackish by the tide. Could this be the original well of Guaire's castle? Nobody would build a castle unless it had within its walls a water supply. And the salmon dams—were they really constructed by someone to trap fish? Or were they the remains of the walls of Guaire's old castle dating from the seventh century?

These were questions which could not be answered without extensive excavation by experts. But there was a hint at the answer in several large holes close to the tiny island revealed by the receding tide. These holes were not rounded but rectangular. Their rock sides were cut as square as boxes. Plainly they were the stone pits from which building material for either Guaire's castle or the later Norman structure had been taken.

But I was concerned with the dishes and Saint Colman. There had been such a man as Colman, but his life is hard

176

to untangle from several contemporaries who had similar names. My information gleaned from the library said that Guaire the Hospitable had given him a piece of land and on it he had built the monastery of Killmacduagh (the Church of the Son of Duagh), which had consisted of seven churches and the inevitable round tower. Colman is buried there.

I went to Killmacduagh to find his grave but of course could not find it. There were many old graves lying under matted grass and weeds—some of them in the ruined, roofless churches, some in the churchyard. There was one large sarcophagus with a carving over it of the crucifixion dating from perhaps the twelfth century. But the epitaph was undecipherable. There was nowhere a single plaque giving either the history of the monastery or marking the grave of the saintly Colman. Some of the graves in the churches

were covered with a layer of cow pads, since respect for the
graves of those long dead is not a trait of the Irish. (In
Kinvara itself I was shown a graveyard some two hundred
years old which was used as a rubbish dump and was foul
with garbage.) At Killmacduagh there was only the usual
irritating notice in Irish warning people against defacing
the buildings.

Frustrated, I returned home, having found nothing tan-
gible about the miracle of the dishes, which I decided was
just a tale invented to illustrate the lavishness of Guaire's
hospitality. Probably, I decided, he had sent an Easter
breakfast to the hermit Colman on the mountain top, and
Irish imagination had woven this into a miracle.

At this time, there was a water shortage in Galway. The
reason there was a water shortage is that many areas of
Galway receive up to eighty inches of rain a year. With
that amount of rain, only an idiot would think of setting up
a large reservoir to save water. However, there having been
little or no rain in July or August, wells were dry and the
well which supplied the houses of Kinvara was so low that
the water coming to household faucets was brackish for the
sea water now flowed into it.

One result was that I had to get drinking water from a
spring and carry it home in buckets. I did this many times,
cursing the improvidence of my countrymen and reflecting
that though I live in Los Angeles, which was once a desert
area with a rainfall of not much over six inches a year, I have
water and to spare readily available in my house.

The spring from which I obtained my water was on the
flank of a stone mountain, reached by a tiny, unpaved road.
One day I inquired idly whether this little road had a name.

"It has," said my informant.

178

"What is the name?"

"Bothar na nias."

Bothar na nias—the Road of the Dishes.

"Is this the road along which the dishes went from Guaire's castle to Saint Colman?" I asked.

"The same."

"And are there on the mountain here the footprints of the horses?"

"Yes, but they are hard to find."

"Do you think that I would find them if I looked?"

"You would. God willing."

But it was Kevin who found them. He called out, "Daddy, come quickly. Here are the horses' hooves." Up I scrambled, and there, in the stone of the mountain, clearly marked, were hoofprints, quite deep, as if the stone had melted and then hardened as related in the legend. I examined them carefully. There could be no mistake about it. Such prints could not be caused by erosion—the shape was too curious. Neither rain nor wind could carve such a set of hooves in the stone of the mountain. They were grouped as if the horses had been attempting to climb the mountain in short leaps, which would be natural in such conditions. They led toward the summit. I made a careful note of the position of the hooves, picking out several markers by which I could find them again, and returned home.

A few days later I took a friend to the mountain to show him the hoofprints. I located my markers. But the prints were gone. I searched and searched and could find not a single one.

My friend was an Irishman, and while I searched, he sat down on a rock and smoked a cigarette.

"I tell you," I said, somewhat nettled by his attitude,

"they were right here. Right in this spot. I must be able to find them again."

"And so you will," said my friend. He took a long pull at his cigarette and looking dreamily out to sea, repeated, "So you will. God willing."

RETURN TO THE WORLD

17. WE were sad when it was time to leave, with a heavy sadness for which no quick cheerful remark could provide the antidote. We went before leaving to the village of Killron to say good-by to Tom and his wife and Tom's brother and the others in the place, and had a final drink at Finherty's bar. Kevin gave his football to Jackeen, who left off holding up his trousers long enough to receive it and say he would keep it for him until we came back again, please God. Most of the men of the village dropped in at Finherty's to say good-by and I had to consume a terrible amount of ginger ale in farewell drinks. Tom's wife hugged Kevin and Tricia as if they were her own and as if she was trying to put into the hugs sufficient of her love to last them until they were grown themselves.

Then we climbed into The Willing Heart and drove to the airport and boarded the plane and fastened our safety belts. And then Ireland, after a little while, floated away from us as it had, but two months previously, floated up toward us through the clouds.

I began to remember some of the little things I had seen

in Ireland and had forgotten for the while—the boy on a bridge talking with his pet crow, the two of them all the while watching the mullet coming up the river; two men on one of the wildest roads in Connemara rolling up big squares of linoleum to put in the back of their van; a nun sitting alone on a hummock in the bogs, looking, presumably, at God; and twenty nuns leaning over a convent wall, faces pink with excitement, as they watched the contestants in the Round-Ireland Bicycle Race wheel by.

I remembered a funeral I had been to with Pat of a man who was the strongest in the whole district. "He carried eight hundred pounds on his back one day," said Pat, "and he was the only man that rode out of the great storm—for the rest of the men in the curraghs were exhausted and were driven onto the rocks, but he rowed for twelve hours and so he lived."

"How long ago was the great storm?" I asked.

"It was about thirty years," said Pat. "When he got ashore he pulled his curragh up into a field and then went to his house and slept for a day and a night."

While I was thinking of this and of three white swans I had seen one day flying over a black lake, Tricia knelt in her seat and addressed the passenger behind us.

"My daddy's a writer," she said. "We're going to California and he's going to write a book about Ireland."

"For the love of God, sit down," I hissed at Tricia.

"Well, it's true," said Tricia, scowling.

"It is not," said Kevin. "That's not why we went to Ireland at all. It was so we could see why he's an Irishman."

"And did you see?" I asked, recalling that this had indeed been the starting point of the adventure.

"Yes," said Kevin, "it's because it's a happy kind of a

place in a sad kind of way." This did not seem to suit him and he tried to improve on it.

"I mean it's just as if it wasn't there at all," he said, eventually.

And, of course, he was perfectly right. The Irish come from a place that isn't really there at all. And I hope it stays that way.

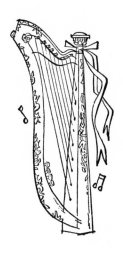